D0324329

THE ALPHABET

OF

ECONOMIC SCIENCE

THE ALPHABET

OF

ECONOMIC SCIENCE

BY

PHILIP H. WICKSTEED

ELEMENTS OF THE THEORY OF VALUE OR WORTH

REPRINTS OF ECONOMIC CLASSICS

AUGUSTUS M. KELLEY · PUBLISHERS
NEW YORK 1970

First Edition 1888

(London: Macmillan & Company Ltd., 1888)

First in Reprints of Economic Classics 1955

Reprinted 1970 by

AUGUSTUS M. KELLEY · PUBLISHERS

REPRINTS OF ECONOMIC CLASSICS

New York   New York   10001

.   .   .   .

S B N   *678 00379 3*

L C N   *56 1926*

.   .   .   .

PRINTED IN THE UNITED STATES OF AMERICA
by SENTRY PRESS, NEW YORK, N. Y. 10019

" Est ergo sciendum, quod quædam sunt, quæ nostræ potestati minime subjacentia, speculari tantummodo possumus, operari autem non, velut Mathematica, Physica, et Divina. Quædam vero sunt quæ nostræ potestati subjacentia, non solum speculari, sed et operari possumus ; et in iis non operatio propter speculationem, sed hæc propter illam adsumitur, quoniam in talibus operatio est finis. Cum ergo materia præsens politica sit, imo fons atque principium rectarum politiarum ; et omne politicum nostræ potestati subjaceat ; manifestum est, quod materia præsens non ad speculationem per prius, sed ad operationem ordinatur. Rursus, cum in operabilibus principium et causa omnium sit ultimus Finis (movet enim primo agentem), consequens est, ut omnis ratio eorum quæ sunt ad Finem, ab ipso Fine sumatur : nam alia erit ratio incidendi lignum propter domum construendam, et alia propter navim. Illud igitur, si quid est, quod sit Finis ultimus Civilitatis humani Generis, erit hoc principium, per quod omnia quæ inferius probanda sunt, erunt manifesta sufficienter."—DANTE.

Be it known, then, that there are certain things, in no degree subject to our power, which we can make the objects of speculation, but not of action. Such are mathematics, physics and theology. But there are some which are subject to our power, and to which we can direct not only our speculations but our actions. And in the case of these, action does not exist for the sake of speculation, but we speculate with a view to action ; for in such matters action is the goal. Since the material of the present treatise, then, is political, nay, is the very fount and starting-point of right polities, and since all that is political is subject to our power, it is obvious that this treatise ultimately concerns conduct rather than speculation. Again, since in all things that can be done the final goal is the general determining principle and cause (for this it is that first stimulates the agent), it follows that the whole rationale of the actions directed to the goal depends upon that goal itself. For the method of cutting wood to build a house is one, to build a ship another. Therefore that thing (and surely there is such a thing) which is the final goal of human society will be the principle by reference to which all that shall be set forth below must be made clear.

PREFACE

DEAR READER—I venture to discard the more stately forms of preface which alone are considered suitable for a serious work, and to address a few words of direct appeal to you.

An enthusiastic but candid friend, to whom I showed these pages in proof, dwelt in glowing terms on the pleasure and profit that my reader would derive from them, "if only he survived the first cold plunge into 'functions.'" Another equally candid friend to whom I reported the remark exclaimed, "*Survive* it indeed! Why, what on earth is to induce him to *take* it?"

Much counsel was offered me as to the best method of inducing him to take this "cold plunge," the substance of which counsel may be found at the beginning of the poems of Lucretius and Tasso, who have given such exquisite expression to the theory of "sugaring the pill" which their works illustrate. But I am no Lucretius, and have no power, even had I the desire to disguise the fact that a firm grasp of the elementary truths of Political Economy cannot be got without the same kind of severe and sustained mental application which is necessary in all other serious studies.

At the same time I am aware that forty pages of almost unbroken mathematics may seem to many readers a most unnecessary introduction to Economics, and it is impossible that the beginner should see their bearing upon the subject until he has mastered and applied them. Some impatience, therefore, may naturally be expected. To remove this impatience, I can but express my own profound conviction that the beginner who has mastered this mathematical introduction will have solved, before he knows that he has even met them, some of the most crucial problems of Political Economy on which the foremost Economists have disputed unavailingly for generations for lack of applying the mathematical method. A glance at the "Index of Illustrations" will show that my object is to bring Economics down from the clouds and make the study throw light on our daily doings and experiences, as well as on the great commercial and industrial machinery of the world. But in order to get this light some mathematical knowledge is needed, which it would be difficult to pick out of the standard treatises as it is wanted. This knowledge I have tried to collect and render accessible to those who dropped their mathematics when they left school, but are still willing to take the trouble to master a plain statement, even if it involves the use of mathematical symbols.

The portions of the book printed in the smaller type should be omitted on a first reading. They generally deal either with difficult portions of the subject that are best postponed till the reader has some idea of the general drift of what he is doing, or else with objections that will probably not present themselves at first, and are better not dealt with till they rise naturally.

The student is strongly recommended to consult the Summary of Definitions and Propositions on pp. 139, 140 at frequent intervals while reading the text.

P. H. W.

INTRODUCTION

On 1st June 1860 Stanley Jevons wrote to his brother Herbert, "During the last session I have worked a good deal at political economy; in the last few months I have fortunately struck out what I have no doubt is *the true Theory of Economy*, so thoroughgoing and consistent, that I cannot now read other books on the subject without indignation."

Jevons was a student at University College at this time, and his new theory failed even to gain him the modest distinction of a class-prize at the summer examination. He was placed third or fourth in the list, and, though much disappointed, comforted himself with the prospect of his certain success when in a few months he should bring out his work and "re-establish the science on a sensible basis." Meanwhile he perceived more and more clearly how fruitful his discovery must prove, and "how the want of knowledge of this determining principle throws the more complicated discussions of economists into confusion."

It was not till 1862 that Jevons threw the main outlines of his theory into the form of a paper, to be read before the British Association. He was fully and most justly conscious of its importance. "Although I know pretty well the paper is perhaps worth all the others that will be read there put together, I cannot pretend to say how it will be received." When the year had but five minutes more to live he wrote of it, "It has seen my theory of economy offered to a learned society (?)

and received without a word of interest or belief. It has convinced me that success in my line of endeavour is even a slower achievement than I had thought."

In 1871, having already secured the respectful attention of students and practical men by several important essays, Jevons at last brought out his *Theory of Political Economy* as a substantive work. It was received in England much as his examination papers at college and his communication to the British Association had been received; but in Italy and in Holland it excited some interest and made converts. Presently it appeared that Professor Walras of Lausanne had been working on the very same lines, and had arrived independently at conclusions similar to those of Jevons. Attention being now well roused, a variety of neglected essays of a like tendency were re-discovered, and served to show that many independent minds had from time to time reached the principle for which Jevons and Walras were contending; and we may now add, what Jevons never knew, that in the very year 1871 the Viennese Professor Menger was bringing out a work which, in complete independence of Jevons and his predecessors, and by a wholly different approach, established the identical theory at which the English and Swiss scholars were likewise labouring.

In 1879 appeared the second edition of Jevons's *Theory of Political Economy*, and now it could no longer be ignored or ridiculed. Whether or not his guiding principle is to win its way to general acceptance and to "re-establish the science on a sensible basis," it has at least to be seriously considered and seriously dealt with.

It is this guiding principle that I have sought to illustrate and enforce in this elementary treatise on the Theory of Value or Worth. Should it be found to meet a want amongst students of economics, I shall hope to follow it by similar introductions to other branches of the science.

I lay no claim to originality of any kind. Those

who are acquainted with the works of Jevons, Walras, Marshall, and Launhardt, will see that I have not only accepted their views, but often made use of their terminology and adopted their illustrations without specific acknowledgment. But I think they will also see that I have copied nothing mechanically, and have made every proposition my own before enunciating it.

I have to express my sincere thanks to Mr. John Bridge, of Hampstead, for valuable advice and assistance in the mathematical portions of my work.

I need hardly add that while unable to claim credit for any truth or novelty there may be in the opinions advocated in these pages, I must accept the undivided responsibility for them.

*** Beginners will probably find it conducive to the comprehension of the argument to omit the small print in the first reading.

N.B.—I have frequently given the formulas of the curves used in illustration. Not because I attach any value or importance to the special forms of the curves, but because I have found by experience that it would often be convenient to the student to be able to calculate for himself any point on the actual curve given in the figures which he may wish to determine for the purpose of checking and varying the hypotheses of the text.

As a rule I have written with a view to readers guiltless of mathematical knowledge (see Preface). But I have sometimes given information in footnotes, without explanation, which is intended only for those who have an elementary knowledge of the higher mathematics.

In conclusion I must apologise to any mathematicians into whose hands this primer may fall for the evidences which they will find on every page of my own want of systematic mathematical training, but I trust they will detect no errors of reasoning or positive blunders.

TABLE OF CONTENTS

I

It is the object of this volume in the first place to explain the meaning and demonstrate the truth of the proposition, that *the value in use and the value in exchange of any commodity are two distinct, but connected, functions of the quantity of the commodity possessed by the persons or the community to whom it is valuable,* and in the second place, so to familiarise the reader with some of the methods and results that necessarily flow from that proposition as to make it impossible for him unconsciously to accept arguments and statements which are inconsistent with it. In other words, I aim at giving what theologians might call a "saving" knowledge of the fundamental proposition of the Theory of Value; for this, but no more than this, is necessary as the first step towards mastering the "alphabet of Economic Science."

When I speak of a "function," I use the word in the mathematical not the physiological sense; and our first business is to form a clear conception of what such a function is.

One quantity, or measurable thing (y), *is a function of another measurable thing* (x), *if any change in x will produce or "determine" a definite corresponding change in y.* Thus the sum I pay for a piece of cloth of given quality is a function of its length, because any alteration in the length purchased will cause a definite corresponding alteration in the sum I have to pay.

If I do not stipulate that the cloth shall be of the same quality in every case, the sum to be paid will still be a function of the length, though not of the length alone, but of the quality also.   For it remains true that an alteration in the length will always produce a definite corresponding alteration in the sum to be paid, although a contemporaneous alteration in the quality may produce another definite alteration (in the same or the opposite sense) at the same time.   In this case the sum to be paid would be "a function of two variables" (see below).   It might still be said, however, without qualification or supplement, that "the sum to be paid is a function of the length;" for the statement, though not complete, would be perfectly correct.   It asserts that every change of length causes a corresponding change in the sum to be paid, and it asserts nothing more.   It is therefore true without qualification.   In this book we shall generally confine ourselves to the consideration of one variable at a time.

So again, if a heavy body be allowed to drop from a height, the longer it has been allowed to fall the greater the space it has traversed, and any change in the time allowed will produce a definite corresponding change in the space traversed.   Therefore the space traversed (say y ft.) is a function of the time allowed (say x seconds).

Or if a hot iron is plunged into a stream of cold water, the longer it is left in the greater will be the fall in its temperature.   The fall in temperature then (say y degrees) is a function of the time of immersion (say x seconds).

The correlative term to "function" is "variable," or, in full, "independent variable."   If y is a function of x, then x is the variable of that function. Thus in the case of the falling body, the time is the variable and the space traversed the function.   When we wish to state that a magnitude is a function of x, without specifying what particular function (i.e. when we wish to say that the value of y depends upon the value of x, and changes with it, without defining the nature or law of its dependence), it is usual to represent the magnitude in question by the symbol $f(x)$ or $\phi(x)$, etc. Thus, " let $y = f(x)$ " would mean " let y be a magnitude which changes when x changes." In the case of the falling body we know that the space traversed, measured in feet, is (approximately) sixteen times the square of the number of seconds during which the body has fallen. Therefore if x be the number of seconds, then y or $f(x)$ equals $16\ x^2$.

Since the statement $y = f(x)$ implies a *definite relation* between the changes in y and the changes in x, it follows that a change in y will determine a corresponding change in x, as well as *vice versâ*. Hence if y is a function of x it follows that x is also a function of y. In the case of the falling body, if $y = 16x^2$, then $x = \dfrac{\sqrt{y}}{4}$.* It is usual to denote inverse functions of this description by the index -1. Thus if $f(x) = y$, then $f^{-1}(y) = x$. In this case $y = 16x^2$, and $f^{-1}(y)$ becomes $f^{-1}(16x^2)$. Therefore $f^{-1}(16x^2) = x$. But $x = \dfrac{\sqrt{16x^2}}{4}$. Therefore $f^{-1}(16x^2) = \dfrac{\sqrt{16x^2}}{4}$. And $16x^2 = y$. Therefore $f^{-1}(y) = \dfrac{\sqrt{y}}{4}$. In like manner $f^{-1}(a) = \dfrac{\sqrt{a}}{4}$; and generally $f^{-1}(x) = \dfrac{\sqrt{x}}{4}$, whatever x may be.

Thus
$$y = f(x) = 16x^2,$$
$$x = f^{-1}(y) = \frac{\sqrt{y}}{4}.$$

(See below, p. 11.)

From the formula $y = f(x) = 16x^2$ we can easily calculate the successive values of $f(x)$ as x increases, *i.e.* the space traversed by the falling body in one, two, three, etc., seconds.

---

* In the abstract $x = \pm \dfrac{\sqrt{y}}{4}$. For $-x$ and x will give the same values of y in $f(x) = 16x^2 = y$; and we shall have $\pm x = \dfrac{\sqrt{y}}{4}$.

$x \quad f(x) = 16x^2$

$0 \quad f(0) = 16 \times 0^2 = \quad 0.$	
$1 \quad f(1) = 16 \times 1^2 = \quad 16$ growth during last second	16
$2 \quad f(2) = 16 \times 2^2 = \quad 64$ „ „	48
$3 \quad f(3) = 16 \times 3^2 = 144$ „ „	80
$4 \quad f(4) = 16 \times 4^2 = 256$ „ „	112
etc. etc. etc. etc.	etc.

In the case of the cooling iron in the stream the time allowed is again the variable, but the function, which we will denote by $\phi(x)$, is not such a simple one, and we need not draw out the details. Without doing so, however, we can readily see that there will be an important difference of character between this function and the one we have just investigated. For the space traversed by the falling body not only grows continually, but grows more in each successive second than it did in the last, as is shown in the last column of the table. Now it is clear that though the cooling iron will always go on getting cooler, yet it will not cool more during each successive second than it did during the last. On the contrary, the fall in temperature of the red-hot iron in the first second will be much greater than the fall in, say, the hundredth second, when the water is only very little colder than the iron ; and the total fall can never be greater than the total difference between the initial temperatures of the iron and the water. This is expressed by saying that the one function $f(x)$, *increases without limit* as the variable, x, increases, and that the other function $\phi(x)$ *approaches a definite limit* as the variable, x, increases. In either case the function is always increased by an increase of the variable, but only in the first case can we make the function as great as we like by increasing the variable sufficiently ; for in the second case there is a certain fixed limit which the function will never reach, however long it continues to increase. If the reader finds this conception difficult or paradoxical, let him consider the series $1 + \frac{1}{2} + \frac{1}{4} + \frac{1}{8} + \frac{1}{16}$, etc., and let $f(x)$ signify the sum of x terms of this series. Then we shall have

x	$f(x)$
1	1.
2	$\frac{3}{2}$ (i.e. $1 + \frac{1}{2}$).
3	$\frac{7}{4}$ (i.e. $1 + \frac{1}{2} + \frac{1}{4}$).
4	$\frac{15}{8}$ (i.e. $1 + \frac{1}{2} + \frac{1}{4} + \frac{1}{8}$).
5	$\frac{31}{16}$ (i.e. $1 + \frac{1}{2} + \frac{1}{4} + \frac{1}{8} + \frac{1}{16}$).
etc.	etc.

Here $f(x)$ is always made greater by increasing x, but however great we make x we shall never make $f(x)$ quite equal to 2. This case furnishes a simple instance of a function which always increases as its variable increases, but yet never reaches a certain fixed limit. The cooling iron presents a more complicated case of such a function.

The two functions we have selected for illustration differ then in this respect, that as the variable (time) increases, the one (space traversed by a falling body) increases without limit, while the other (fall of temperature in the iron) though always increasing yet approaches a fixed limit. But $f(x)$ and $\phi(x)$ resemble each other in this, that they both of them always increase (and never decrease) as the variable increases.

There are, however, many functions of which this cannot be said. For instance, let a body be projected vertically upwards, and let the height at which we find it at any given moment be regarded as a function of the time which has elapsed since its projection. It is obvious that at first the body will rise (doing work against gravitation), and the function (height) will increase as the variable (time) increases. But the initial energy of the body cannot hold out and do work against gravitation for ever, and after a time the body will rise no higher, and will then begin to fall, in obedience to the still acting force of gravitation. Then a further increase

of the variable (time) will cause, not an increase, but a
decrease in the function (height). Thus, as the variable
increases, the function will at first increase with it, and
then decrease.

To recapitulate : one thing is a function of another
if it varies with it, whether increasing as it increases or
decreasing as it increases, or changing at a certain point
or points from the one relation to the other.

We have already reached a point at which we can
attach a definite meaning to the proposition : *The value-
in-use of any commodity to an individual is a function of the
quantity of it he possesses*, and as soon as we attach a
definite meaning to it, we perceive its truth. For by
the value-in-use of a commodity to an individual, we
mean the total worth of that commodity to him, for his
own purposes, or the sum of the advantages he derives
immediately from its possession, excluding the advantages
he anticipates from exchanging it for something else.
Now it is clear that this sum of advantages is greater
or less according to the quantity of the commodity the
man possesses. It is not the same for different quantities. The value-in-use of two blankets, that is to say
the total direct service rendered by them, or the sum of
direct advantages I derive from possessing them, differs
from the value-in-use of one blanket. If you increase
or diminish my supply of blankets you increase or
diminish the sum of direct advantages I derive from
them. The value-in-use of my blankets, then, is a
function of the number (or quantity) I possess. Or if
we take some commodity which we are accustomed to
think of as acquired and used at a certain rate rather than
in certain absolute quantities, the same fact still appears.
The value-in-use of one gallon of water a day, that is to
say the sum of direct advantages I derive from com-
manding it, differs from the value-in-use of a pint a day
or of two gallons a day. The sum of direct advantages
which I derive from half a pound of butcher's meat a

day is something different from that which I should
derive from either an ounce or a whole carcase per day.
In other words, *the sum of the advantages I derive from
the direct use or consumption of a commodity is a function
of its quantity, and increases or decreases as that quantity
changes.*

Two points call for attention here. In the first place,
there are many commodities which we are not in the habit
of thinking of as possessed in varying quantities ; or at any
rate, we usually think of the services they render as functions of some other variable than their quantity. For instance, a watch that is a good time-keeper renders a greater
sum of services to its possessor than a bad one ; but it seems
an unwarrantable stretch of language to say that the owner
of a good watch has " a greater amount or quantity of watch "
than the owner of a bad one. It is a little more reasonable,
though still hardly admissible, to say that the one has "more
time-keeping apparatus " than the other. But, as the reader
will remember, we have already seen that a function may
depend on two or more variables (p. 2), and if we consider
watches of different qualities as one and the same commodity,
then we must say that the most important variable is the
quality of the watch ; but it will still be true that two
watches of the same quality would, as a rule, perform a
different (and a greater) service for a man than one watch ;
for most men who have only one have experienced temporary
inconvenience when they have injured it, and would have
been very glad of another in reserve. Even in this case,
therefore, the sum of advantages derived from the commodity
" watches " is a function of the quantity as well as the quality.
Moreover, the distinction is of no theoretical importance, for
the propositions we establish concerning value-in-use as a
function of quantity will be equally true of it as a function
of quality ; and indeed "quality " in the sense of "excel-
lence," being conceivable as "more " or "less," is obviously
itself a quantity of some kind.

The second consideration is suggested by the frequent use
of the phrase " *sum of advantages* " as a paraphrase of " *worth* "
or "*value-in-use.*" What are we to consider an " advantage "?

It is usual to say that in economics everything which a man wants must be considered "useful" to him, and that the word must therefore be emptied of its moral significance. In this sense a pint of beer is more "useful" than a gimlet to a drunken carpenter. And, in like manner, a wealthier person of similar habits would be said to derive a greater "sum of advantages" from drinking two bottles of wine at dinner than from drinking two glasses. In either case, we are told, that is "useful" which ministers to a desire, and it is an "advantage" to have our desires gratified. Economics, it is said, have nothing to do with ethics, since they deal, not with the legitimacy of human desires, but with the means of satisfying them by human effort. In answer to this I would say that if and in so far as economics have nothing to do with ethics, economists must refrain from using ethical words ; for such epithets as "useful" and "advantageous" will, in spite of all definitions, continue to carry with them associations which make it both dangerous and misleading to apply them to things which are of no real use or advantage. I shall endeavour, as far as I can, to avoid, or at least to minimise, this danger. I am not aware of any recognised word, however, which signifies the quality of being desired. "Desirableness" conveys the idea that the thing not only is but deserves to be desired. "Desiredness" is not English, but I shall nevertheless use it as occasion may require. "Gratification" and "satisfaction" are expressions morally indifferent, or nearly so, and may be used instead of "advantage" when we wish to denote the result of obtaining a thing desired, irrespective of its real effect on the weal or woe of him who secures it.

Let us now return to the illustration of the body projected vertically upwards at a given velocity. In this case the time allowed is the variable, and the height of the body is the function. Taking the rough approximation with which we are familiar, which gives sixteen feet as the space through which a body will fall from rest in the first second, and supposing that the velocity with which the body starts is a ft. per second, we learn by experiment, and might deduce from more general laws, that we shall have $y = ax - 16x^2$, where x is the number of seconds allowed, and y is the height of the body at the end of x seconds. If $a = 128$, *i.e.* if the body starts at a velocity of 128 ft. per second, we shall have

$$y = 128x - 16x^2.$$

In such an expression the figures 128 and -16 are called the *constants*, because they remain the same throughout the investigation, while x and y change. If we wish to indicate the general type of the relationship between x and $f(x)$ or y without determining its details, we may express the constants by letters. Thus $y = ax + bx^2$ would determine the general character of the function, and by choosing 128 and -16 as the constants we get a definite specimen of the type, which absolutely determines the relation between x and y. Thus $y = ax + bx^2$ is the general formula for the distance traversed in x seconds by a body that starts with a given velocity and works directly with or against a constant force. If the constant force is gravitation, b must equal 16 ; if the body is to work against (not with) gravitation the sign of b must be negative. If the initial velocity of the body is 128 ft. per second, a must equal 128.

By giving successive values of 1, 2, 3, etc. to x in the expression $128x - 16x^2$, we find the height at which the body will be at the end of the 1, 2, 3, etc. seconds.

x	$f(x) = 128x - 16x^2$
0	$f(0) = 128 \times 0 - 16 \times 0^2 = 0$
1	$f(1) = 128 \times 1 - 16 \times 1^2 = 112$
2	$f(2) = 128 \times 2 - 16 \times 2^2 = 192$
3	$f(3) = 128 \times 3 - 16 \times 3^2 = 240$
etc. etc.	etc. etc.

Now this relation between the function and the variable may be represented graphically by the well-known method of measuring the *variable* along a base line, starting from a given point, and measuring the *function* vertically upwards from that line, negative quantities in either case being measured in the opposite direction to that selected for positive quantities. To apply this method we must select our unit of length and then give it a fixed interpretation in the quantities we are dealing with. Suppose we say that a unit measured along the base line OX in Fig. 1 shall represent one second, and that a unit measured vertically from OX in the direction OY shall represent 10 ft. We may then represent the connection between the height at which the body is to be found and the lapse of time since its projection by a curved line. We shall proceed thus. Let us suppose a movable button to slip along the line OX, bearing with it as it moves along a vertical line (parallel to OY) indefinitely extended both upwards and downwards. The movement of this button (which we may regard as a point, without magnitude, and which we may call a "bearer") along OX will represent the lapse of time. The lapse of one second, therefore, will be represented by the movement of the bearer one unit to the right of O. Now by this time the body will have risen 112 ft., which will be represented by 11·2 units, measured upwards on the vertical line carried by the bearer. This will bring us to the point indicated on Fig. 1 by P_1. Let us mark this point and then slip on the bearer through another unit. This will represent a total lapse of two seconds, by which time the body will have reached a height of 192 ft., which will be represented by 19·2 units measured on the vertical. This will bring us to P_2. In P_1 and P_2 we have now representations of two points in the history of the projectile. P_1 is distant one unit from the line OY and 11·2 units from OX, i.e. it represents a movement from O of 1 unit in the direction OX (time, or x), and of 11·2 units in the direction of OY (height, or y). This indicates that 11·2 is the value of y which corresponds to the value 1 of x. In like manner the position of P_2 indicates that 19·2 is the value of y that corresponds to the value 2 of x. Now, instead of finding an

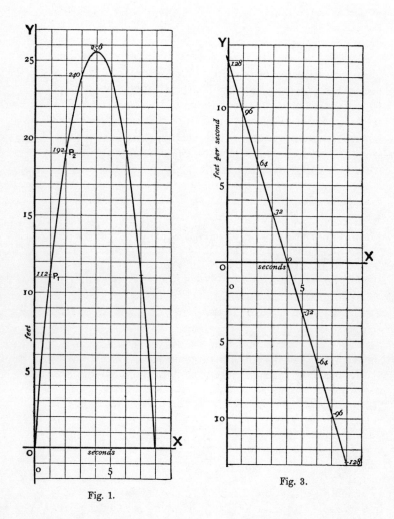

Fig. 1.

Fig. 3.

indefinite number of these points, let us suppose that as
the bearer moves continuously (*i.e.* without break) along
OX a pointed pencil is continuously drawn along the
vertical, keeping exact pace, to scale, with the moving
body, and therefore always registering its height,—a unit
of length on the vertical representing 10 ft. Obviously the
point of the pencil will trace a continuous curve, the course
of which will be determined by two factors, the horizontal
factor representing the lapse of time and the vertical
factor representing the movement of the body, and if we
take any point whatever on this curve it will represent
a point in the history of the projectile ; its distance
from OY giving a certain point of time and its distance
from OX the corresponding height.

Such a curve is represented by Fig. 1. We have
seen how it is to be formed ; and when formed it is to
be read thus : If we push the bearer along OX, then for
every length measured along OX the curve cuts off a corresponding length on the vertical, which we will call the
" vertical intercept." That is to say, for every value of x
(time) the curve marks a corresponding value of y (height).

OX is called " the axis of x," because x is measured
along it or in its direction. OY is, for like reason,
called " the axis of y."

We have seen that if y is a function of x then it follows
that x is also a function of y (p. 3). Hence the curve we
have traced may be regarded as representing $x = f^{-1}(y)$ no
less than $y = f(x)$. If we move our bearer along OY to
represent the height attained, and make it carry a line
parallel to OX, then the curve will cut off a length indicating
the time that corresponds to that height. It will be seen
that there are two such lengths of x corresponding to every
length of y between 0 and 25·6, one indicating the moment
at which the body will reach the given height as it ascends,
and the other the moment at which it returns to the same
height in its descent.

As an exercise in the notation, let the student follow this
series of axiomatic identical equations : given $y = f(x)$, then

$xy = f(x) x = f^{-1}(y) \; f(x) = f^{-1}(y)y.$ Also $f^{-1}[f(x)] = x$ and $f[f^{-1}(y)] = y.$

It must be carefully noted that the curve *does not give us a picture of the course of the projectile.* We have supposed the body to be projected vertically upwards, and its course will therefore be a straight line, and would be marked by the movement of the pencil up and down the vertical, taken alone, and not in combination with the movement of the vertical itself; just as the time would be marked by the movement of the pencil, with the bearer, along OX, taken alone. In fact the best way to conceive of the curve is to imagine one bearer moving along OX and marking the time, to scale, while a second bearer moves along OY and marks the height of the body, to scale, while the pencil point *follows the direction and speed of both of them at once.* The pencil point, it will be seen, will always be at the intersection of the vertical carried by one bearer and the horizontal carried by the other. Thus it will be quite incorrect and misleading to call the curve "a curve of height," and equally but not more so to call it "a curve of time." Both height and time are represented by straight lines, and the curve is a "curve of height-and-time," or "a curve of time-and-height," that is to say, *a curve which shows the history of the connection between height and time.*

And again the scales on which time and height are measured are altogether indifferent, as long as we read our curve by the same scale on which we construct it. The student should accustom himself to draw a curve on a number of different scales and observe the wonderful changes in its appearance, while its meaning, however tested, always remains the same.

All these points are illustrated in Fig. 2, where the very same history of the connection between time and height in a body projected vertically upwards at 128 ft. per second is traced for four seconds and 256 ft., but the height is drawn on the scale 50 ft. $\frac{1}{6}$ in. instead of 10 ft. $\frac{1}{6}$ in. It shows us that the lines representing space and those representing time enter into the construction of the curve on precisely the same footing. The curve, if drawn, would therefore be neither a curve of time nor a curve of height, but a curve of time-and-height.

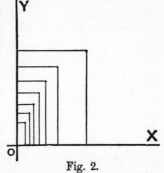

Fig. 2.

The curve then, is not a picture of the course of the projectile in space, and a similar curve might equally well represent the history of a phenomenon that has no course in space and is independent of time.

For instance, the expansion of a metal bar under tension is a function of the degree of tension; and a testing machine may register the connection between the tension and expansion upon a curve. The tension is the variable x (measured in tons, per inch cross-section of specimen tested, and drawn on axis of x to the scale of, say, seven tons to the inch), and the expansion is $f(x)$ or y (measured in inches, and drawn on axis of y, say to the natural scale, $1:1$).*

The tension and expansion, then, are indicated by straight lines, constantly changing in length, but the history of their connection is a curve. It is not a curve

---

* If we take tension (the variable) along y, and expansion (the function) along x, the theory is of course the same. As a fact, it is usual in testing-machines to regard the tension as measured on the vertical and the expansion on the horizontal. It is only a question of how the paper is held in the hand, and the reader will do well to throw the curve of time-and-height also, on its side, read its x as y and its y as x, and learn with ease and certainty to read off the same results as before. This will be useful in finally dispelling the illusion (that reasserts itself with some obstinacy) that the figure represents the course of the projectile. The figures may also be varied by being drawn from right to left instead of from left to right, etc. It is of great importance not to become dependent on any special convention as to the position, etc. of the curves.

of expansion or a curve of tension, but a curve of tension-and-expansion.

Or again, the pleasurable sensation of sitting in a Turkish bath is a function, amongst other things, of the temperature to which the bath is raised. If we treat that temperature as the variable, and measure its increase by slipping the bearer along the base line OX, then the whole body of facts concerning the varying degrees of pleasure to be derived from the bath, according to its varying degrees of heat, might be represented by a curve, which would be in some respects analogous to that represented on Fig. 1 ; for, as we measure the rise of temperature by moving the bearer along our base line, we shall, up to a certain point, read our increasing sense of luxury on the increasing length of the vertical intercepted by a rising curve, after which the increasing temperature will be accompanied by a decreasing sense of enjoyment, till at last the enjoyment will sink to zero, and, if the heat is still raised, will become a rapidly increasing negative quantity. · Thus :

If we have a function (of one variable), then whatever the nature of the function may be, the connection between the function and the variable is theoretically capable of representation by a curve. And since we have seen that the total satisfaction we derive from the enjoyment or use of any commodity is a function of the quantity we possess (*i.e.* changes in magnitude as the quantity increases or decreases), it follows that *a curve must theoretically exist which assigns to every conceivable quantity of a given commodity the corresponding total satisfaction to be derived by a given man from its use or possession ;* or, in other words, *the connection between the total satisfaction derived from the enjoyment of a commodity and the quantity of the commodity so enjoyed is theoretically capable of being represented by a curve.* Now this "total satisfaction derived" is what economists call the "total utility," or the "value-in-use" of a commodity. The conclusion we have reached may therefore be stated thus : Since the value-in-use of a commodity varies with the quantity of the commodity used, *the connection between the quantity of a commodity possessed and its value-in-use may, theoretically, be represented by a curve.*

Here an initial difficulty presents itself. To imagine the construction of such a curve as even theoretically possible, we should have to conceive the theoretical possibility of fixing a unit of satisfaction, by which to measure off satisfactions two, three, four times as great as the standard unit, on our vertical line, just as we measured tens of feet on it in Fig. 1. We shall naturally be led in the course of our inquiry to deal with this objection, which is not really formidable (see p. 52); and it is only mentioned here to show that it has not been overlooked. Meanwhile, it may be observed that since satisfaction is certainly capable of being "more" or "less," and since the mind is capable of estimating one satisfaction as "greater than" or "equal to" another, it cannot be theoretically impossible to conceive of such a thing as an accurate measurement of satisfaction, even though its practical measurement should always remain as vague as that of heat was when the thermometer was not yet invented.

We may go a step farther, and may say that, if curves representing the connection between these economic functions (values-in-use) and their variables (quantities of commodity) could be actually drawn out, they would, at any rate in many cases, present an important point of analogy with our curve in Fig. 1; for they would first ascend and then descend, and ultimately pass below zero. As the quantity of any commodity in our possession increases we gradually approach the point at which it has conferred upon us the full satisfaction we are capable of deriving from it; after this a larger stock is not in any degree desired, and would not add anything to our satisfaction. In a word, we have as much as we want, and would not take any more at a gift. The function has then reached its maximum value, corresponding to the highest point on the curve.

If the commodity is still thrust upon us beyond this point of complete satisfaction, the further increments become, as a rule, *discommodious*, and the excessive quantity *diminishes* the total satisfaction we derive from possessing the commodity, till at length a point is reached at which the inconvenience of the excessive supply neutralises the whole of the advantage derived from that part which we can enjoy, and we would just as soon go without it altogether as have so far too much of a good thing.   If the supply is still increased, the net result is a balance of inconvenience, and (if shut up to the alternative of *all* or *none*) we should, on the whole, be the gainers if relieved of the advantage and disadvantage alike.   The heat of a Turkish bath has already given us one instance ; and for another we may take butcher's meat.   Most of us derive (or suppose ourselves to derive) considerable satisfaction from the consumption of fresh meat.   The sum of satisfaction increases as the amount of meat increases up to a point roughly fixed by the popular estimate at half to three-quarters of a pound per diem.   Then we have enough, and if we were required to consume or otherwise personally dispose of a larger amount, the inconvenience of eating, burying, burning, or otherwise getting rid of the surplus, or the unutterable consequences of failing to do so, would partially neutralise the pleasure and advantage of eating the first half pound, till at some point short of a hundredweight of fresh meat per head per diem we should (if shut in to the alternative of all or none) regretfully embrace vegetarianism as the lesser evil.   In this case the curve connecting the value-in-use of meat with its quantity would rise as the supply of meat, measured along the base line, increased until, say at half a pound a day, it reached its maximum elevation, indicating that up to that point more meat meant more satisfaction, after which the curve would begin to descend, indicating that additional supplies of meat would be worse than useless, and would tend to neutralise the satisfaction derived from the portion really desired, and to reduce the total gratification conferred, till at a certain point the curve would cross the base line, indicating that so much meat as that (if we were obliged to take all or none) would be just as bad as none at all, and that if more yet were thrust upon us it would on the whole be *worse* than having none.

Though practically we are almost always concerned with commodities our desire for which is not fully satisfied, that is to say, with the portions of our curves which are still ascending, yet it is highly important, as a matter of theory, to realise the fact that curves of quantity-and-value-in-use must always *tend* to reach a maximum somewhere, and that as a rule they would actually reach that maximum if the variable (measured along the axis of x) were made large enough, and would then descend if the variable were still further increased ; or in other words, that there is hardly any commodity of which we might not conceivably have enough and too much, and even if there be such a commodity its increase would still *tend* to produce satiety (compare p. 5). Some difficulty is often felt in fully grasping this very simple and elementary fact, because we cannot easily divest our minds in imagination of the conditions to which we are practically accustomed. Thus we may find that our minds refuse to isolate the *direct* use of commodities and to contemplate that alone (though it is of this direct use only that we are at present speaking), and persist, when we are off our guard, in readmitting the idea that we might exchange what we cannot use ourselves for something we want. A man will say, for instance, if confronted with the illustration of fresh meat which I have used above, that he would very gladly receive a hundred-weight of fresh meat a-day and would still want more, because he could sell what he did not need for himself. This is of course beside the mark, since our contention is that the *direct value-in-use* of an article always tends to reach a maximum ; but in order to assist the imagination it may be well to take a case in which a whole community may suffer from having too much of a good thing, so that the confusing side-lights of possible exchange may not divert the attention.

Rain, in England at least, is an absolute necessary of life, but if the rainfall is too heavy we derive less benefit from it than if it is normal. Every extra inch of rainfall then becomes a very serious discommodity, reducing the total utility or satisfaction-derived to something lower than it would have been had the rain been less ; and it is conceivable that in certain districts the rain might produce floods that would drown the inhabitants or isolate them, in inaccessible islands, till they died of starvation, thus cancelling the whole of the advantages it confers and making their absolute sum zero.

Another class of objections is, however, sometimes raised. We are told that there are some things, notably money, of which the ordinary man could never have as much as he wanted ; and daily experience shows us that so far from an increased supply of money tending to satisfy the desire for it, the more men have the more they want. This objection is based on a loose use of the phrase "more money." Let us take any definite sum, say £1, and ask what effort or privation a man will be willing to face in order that he may secure it. We shall find, of course, that if a man has a hundred thousand a-year he will be willing to make none but the very smallest effort in order to get a pound more, whereas if the same man only has thirty shillings a-week he will do a good deal to get an extra pound. It is true that the millionaire may still exert himself to get more money ; but to induce him to do so the prospect of gain must be much greater than was necessary when he was a comparatively poor man. He does not want *the same sum of money* as much as he did when he was poor, but he sees the possibility of getting a very large sum, and wants that as much as he used to want a small one. All other objections and apparent exceptions will be found to yield in like manner to careful and accurate consideration.

It is true, however, that a man may form instinctive habits of money-making which are founded on no rational principle, and are difficult to include in any rationale of action ; but even in these cases the action of our law is only complicated by combination with others, not really suspended.

It is also true that the very fact of our having a thing may develop our taste for it and make us want more ; but this, too, is quite consistent with our theory, and will be duly provided for hereafter (p. 63).

Enough has now been said in initial explanation of a curve in general, and specifically a curve that first ascends and then descends, as an appropriate means of representing the connection between the quantity of a commodity and its value-in-use, or the total satisfaction it confers.

But if we return once more to Fig. 1, and recollect that the curve there depicted is a curve of time-and-height, representing the connection between the elevation a body has attained (function) and the time that has elapsed since its projection (variable), we are reminded that there is another closely-connected function of the same variable, with which we are all familiar. We are accustomed to ask of a body falling from rest not only how far it will have travelled in so many seconds, but *at what rate it will be moving* at any given time. And so, of a body projected vertically upwards we ask not only at what height will it be at the end of x seconds, but also *at what rate will it then be rising*. Let us pause for a moment to inquire exactly what we mean by saying that at a given moment a body, the velocity of which is constantly changing, is moving "at the rate" of, say, y feet per second. We mean that if, at that moment, all causes which *modify* the movement of the body were suddenly to become inoperative, and it were to move on solely under the impulse already operative, it would then move y feet in every second, and, consequently, ay feet in a seconds. In the case of Fig. 1 the modifying force is the action of gravitation, and what we mean by the rate at which the body is moving at any moment is the rate at which it would move, from that moment onwards, if from that moment the action of gravitation ceased to be operative.

As a matter of fact it never moves through any space, however small, at the rate we assign, because modifying causes are at work *continuously* (*i.e.* without intervals and without jerks), so that the velocity is never uniform over any fraction of time or space, however small.

When we speak of rate of movement "at a point," then, we are using an abbreviated expression for the rate of movement which would set in at that point if all modifying causes abruptly ceased to act thenceforth.

For instance, if we say that a body falling from rest has acquired a velocity of 32 feet per second when it has been falling for one second, we mean that if, after acting for one second, terrestrial gravitation should then cease to act, the body would thenceforth move 32 feet in every second.

It follows, then, that the departures from this ideal rate spring from the continuous action of the modifying cause, and will be greater or smaller according as the action of that cause has been more or less considerable ; and since the cause (in this instance) acts uniformly in time, it will act more in more time and less in less. Hence, the less the time we allow after the close of one second the more nearly will the rate at every moment throughout that time (and therefore the average rate during that time) conform to the rate of 32 feet per second. And in fact we find that if we calculate (by the formula $s = 16x^2$) the space traversed between the close of the first second and some subsequent point of time, then the smaller the time we allow the more nearly does the average rate throughout that time become 32 ft. per second. Thus—

					Body falls	Average rate per sec.
Between 1 sec. and 2	sec.	48 ft.	48 ft.
,,	1	,,	$1\frac{1}{2}$	,,	20 ,,	40 ,,
,,	1	,,	$1\frac{1}{4}$	,,	9 ,,	36 ,,
,,	1	,,	$1\frac{1}{8}$	,,	$\frac{17}{4}$,,	34 ,,
,,	1	,,	$1\frac{1}{16}$	,,	$\frac{33}{16}$,,	33 ,,
,,	1	,,	$1\frac{1}{32}$	,,	$\frac{65}{64}$,,	32 5

and the average rate between 1 second and $1 + \dfrac{1}{z}$ second may be made as near 32 ft. a second as we like, by making z large enough. This is usually expressed by saying that the average rate between 1 second and $\dfrac{z+1}{z}$ seconds becomes 32 ft. per second *in the limit*, as z becomes greater, or the time allowed smaller.

We may, therefore, define "rate at a point" as the "*limit of the average rate between that point and a subsequent point, as the distance between the two points decreases.*"

With this explanation we may speak of the rate at which the projected body is moving as a function of the time that has elapsed since its projection ; for obviously the rate changes with the time, and that is all that is needed to justify us in regarding the time that elapses as a variable and the rate of movement as a function of that variable. Let us go on then, to consider the relation of this new function of the time elapsed to the function we have already considered. We will call the first function $f(x)$ and the second function $f'(x)$. Then we shall have $x =$ the lapse of time since the projection of the body, measured in seconds ; $f(x) =$ the height attained by the body in x seconds, measured in feet ; $f'(x) =$ the rate at which the body is rising after x seconds, measured in feet per second.

It will be observed that x must be positive, for we have no data as to the history of the body *before* its projection, and if x were negative that would mean that the lapse of time since the projection was negative, *i.e.* that the projection was still in the future. On the other hand, $f(x) = 128x - 16x^2$ will become negative as soon as $16x^2$ is greater than $128x$, *i.e.* as soon as $16x$ is greater than 128, or x greater than $\frac{128}{16} = 8$; which means that after eight seconds the body will not only have passed its greatest height but will already have fallen below the point from which it was originally

projected, so that the "height" at which it is now found, *i.e.*
$f(x)$, will be negative. Again $f'(x)$, or the rate at which the
body is "rising," will become negative as soon as the maximum height is passed, for then the body will be rising
negatively, *i.e.* falling.

We have now to examine the connection between
$f(x)$ and $f'(x)$. Our common phraseology will help us
to understand it. Thus: $f(x)$ expresses the height of
the body at any moment, $f'(x)$ expresses the rate at which
the body is rising; but the rate at which it is rising is
the rate at which its height, or $f(x)$, is increasing. That is,
$f'(x)$ represents the rate which $f(x)$ is increasing. A glance
at Fig. 1 will suffice to show that this rate is not uniform
throughout the course of the projectile. At first the
moving body rises, or increases its height, rapidly, then
less rapidly, then not at all, then negatively—that is to
say, it begins to fall. This, as we have seen, may be
expressed in two ways. We may say $f(x)$ [= the
height] first increases rapidly, then slowly, then negatively, or we may say $f'(x)$ [= the rate of rising] is first
great, then small, then negative.

Formula: $f'(x)$ *represents the rate at which $f(x)$
grows.*

It is obvious then that some definite relation exists
between $f(x)$ and $f'(x)$, and Newton and Leibnitz discovered the nature of that relation and established rules
by which, if any function whatever, $f(x)$, be given, another
function $f'(x)$ may be derived from it which shall
indicate the rate at which it is growing.

This second function is called the "*first derived function,*"
or the "*differential coefficient*"* of the original function, and if
the original function is called $f(x)$, it is usual to represent the
first derived function by $f'(x)$. In some cases it is possible
to perform the reverse operation, and if a function be given,
say $\phi(x)$, to find another function such that $\phi(x)$ shall

---

* See p. 31.

represent the rate of its increase.* This function is then
called the "*integral*" of $\phi(x)$, and is written $\int_0^x \phi(x)dx$. Thus,
if we start with $f(x)$, find the function which represents the
rate of its growth and call it $f'(x)$, and then starting with
$f'(x)$ find a function whose rate of growth is $f'(x)$ and call
it $\int_0^x f'(x)dx$, we shall obviously have $\int_0^x f'(x)dx = f(x)$.

The only flaw in the argument is that it assumes there to
be only one function of x which increases at the rate indicated
by $f'(x)$, and therefore assumes that if we find *any* function
$\int_0^x f'(x)dx$ which increases at that rate, it must necessarily be
the function, $f(x)$, which we already know does increase at that
rate. This is not strictly true, and $\int_0^x f'(x)dx$ is, therefore, an
indeterminate symbol, which represents $f(x)$ and also certain
other functions of x, which resemble $f(x)$ in all respects save
one, which one will not in any way affect our inquiries. As
far as any properties we shall have to consider are concerned,
we may regard the equation

$$\int_0^x f'(x)dx = f(x)$$

as absolute.

In the case we are now considering $f(x)$ is $128x - 16x^2$,
and an application of Newton's rules will tell us that
$f'(x)$ is $128 - 32x$. That is to say, if we are told that
x being the number of seconds since the projection, the
height of the body in feet is always $128x - 16x^2$ for all
values of x, then we know by the rules, without further
experiment, that the rate at which its height is increasing will always be $128 - 32x$ ft.- per - second, for all
values of x. But the rate at which the height is
increasing is the rate at which the body is rising, so
that $128 - 32x$ is the formula which will tell us the
rate at which the body is rising after the lapse of x
seconds.

---

* Such a function always exists, but we cannot always "find" it,
i.e. express it conveniently in finite algebraical notation.

$x=$ number of seconds since the projection.	$f'(x) = 128 - 32\,x =$	Rate at which the body is rising, in feet-per-second.
0	$f'(0) = 128 - 32 \times 0 =$	128
1	$f'(1) = 128 - 32 \times 1 =$	96
2	$f'(2) = 128 - 32 \times 2 =$	64
3	$f'(3) = 128 - 32 \times 3 =$	32
4	$f'(4) = 128 - 32 \times 4 =$	0
5	$f'(5) = 128 - 32 \times 5 =$	$- 32$
6	$f'(6) = 128 - 32 \times 6 =$	$- 64$
7	$f'(7) = 128 - 32 \times 7 =$	$- 96$
8	$f'(8) = 128 - 32 \times 8 =$	$- 128$
etc.	etc. etc.	etc.

Now the connection between $f'(x)$ and x can be represented graphically, just as the connection between $f(x)$ and x was. It must be represented by a curve (in this case a straight line), which makes the vertical intercept 12·8 (representing 128 ft. per second), when the bearer is at the origin (*i.e.* when x is 0), making it 9·6 when the bearer has been moved through one unit to the right of the origin (or when x is 1), and so forth. It is given in Fig. 3 (p. 9), and registers all the facts drawn out in our table, together with all the intermediate facts connected with them. If we wish to read this curve, and to know at what rate the body will be rising after, say, one and a half seconds, we suppose our bearer to be pushed half-way between 1 and 2 on our base line, and then running our eye up the vertical line it carries till it is intercepted by the curve, we find that the vertical intercept measures 8 units. This means that the rate at which the body is rising, one and a half seconds after its projection, is 80 ft. per second.

No attempt will be made here to demonstrate, even in a simple case, the algebraical rules by which the derived functions are obtained from the original ones; but it may be well to show in some little detail, by geometrical methods, the true nature of the connection between a function and its derived function, and the possibility of passing from the one to the other.*

Suppose $OP_1P_2P_3$ in Fig. 4 to be a curve representing the connection of $f(x)$ and x. We may again suppose $f(x)$ to represent the amount of work done against some constant force, in which case it will conform to the type $y = f(x) = ax - bx^2$. The curve in the figure is drawn to the formula

$$f(x) = 2x - \frac{x^2}{8}, \text{ where } a = 2, \ b = \tfrac{1}{8}.$$

This will give the following pairs of corresponding values:—

x	$f(x)\ =\ 2x - \dfrac{x^2}{8}\ =\ y.$	Growth for last unit of increase of x.
0	$f(0) = 2 \times 0 - \frac{0}{8} = 0.$	
1	$f(1) = 2 \times 1 - \frac{1}{8} = 1\frac{7}{8}$	$\frac{15}{8}$
2	$f(2) = 2 \times 2 - \frac{4}{8} = 3\frac{1}{2}$	$\frac{13}{8}$
3	$f(3) = 3 \times 2 - \frac{9}{8} = 4\frac{7}{8}$	$\frac{11}{8}$
4	$f(4) = 4 \times 2 - \frac{16}{8} = 6$	$\frac{9}{8}$
5	$f(5) = 5 \times 2 - \frac{25}{8} = 6\frac{7}{8}$	$\frac{7}{8}$
6	$f(6) = 6 \times 2 - \frac{36}{8} = 7\frac{1}{2}$	$\frac{5}{8}$
7	$f(7) = 7 \times 2 - \frac{49}{8} = 7\frac{7}{8}$	$\frac{3}{8}$
8	$f(8) = 8 \times 2 - \frac{64}{8} = 8$	$\frac{1}{8}$
9	$f(9) = 9 \times 2 - \frac{81}{8} = 7\frac{7}{8}$	$-\frac{1}{8}$
etc.	etc. etc.	etc.

It is clear from an inspection of the curve and from the last column in our table that the rate at which $f(x)$ or y increases per unit increase of x is not uniform throughout its history. While x increases from 0 to 1, y grows nearly two units, but while x increases from 7 to 8, y only grows one eighth of a unit. Now we want to construct a curve on which we can read off the rate at which y is growing at any point of its history. For instance, if y represents the height

---

* The student who finds this note difficult to understand is recommended not to spend much time over it till he has studied the rest of the book.

of a body doing work against gravitation (say rising), we want to construct a curve which shall tell us at what rate the height is increasing at any moment, *i.e.* at what rate the body is rising.

Now since the increase of the function is represented by the rising of the curve, the rate at which the function is increasing is the same thing as the rate at which the curve is rising, and this is the same thing as the steepness of the curve.

Again, common sense seems to tell us (and I shall presently show that it may be rigorously proved) that the steepness of the tangent, or line touching the curve, at any point is the same thing as the steepness of the curve at that point. Thus in Fig. 4, R_1P_1 (the tangent at P_1) is steeper than R_2P_2 (the tangent at P_2), and that again is steeper than $R_3 P_3$ (the tangent at P_3), which last indeed has no steepness at all ; and obviously the curve too is steeper at P_1 than at P_2, and has no steepness at all at P_3.

But we can go farther than this and can get a precise numerical expression for the steepness of the tangent at any point P, by measuring how many times the line QP contains the line RQ (Q being the point at which the perpendicular from any point, P, cuts the axis of x, and R the point at which the tangent to the curve, at the same point P, cuts the same axis). For since QP represents the total upward movement accomplished by passing from R to P, while RQ represents the total forward movement, obviously QP : RQ = ratio of upward movement to forward movement = steepness of tangent.

But steepness of tangent at P = steepness of curve at P = rate at which y is growing at P. To find the rate at which y is growing at P_1, P_2, P_3, etc. we must therefore find the ratios $\dfrac{Q_1 P_1}{R_1 Q_1}$, $\dfrac{Q_2 P_2}{R_2 Q_2}$, $\dfrac{Q_3 P_3}{R_3 Q_3}$, etc. But if we take r_1, r_2, r_3, etc. each one unit to the left of Q_1, Q_2, Q_3, etc. and draw $r_1 p_1$, $r_2 p_2$, $r_3 p_3$, etc. parallel severally to R_1P_1, R_2P_2, R_3P_3 etc., then by similar triangles we shall have

$$\frac{Q_1P_1}{R_1Q_1}=\frac{Q_1p_1}{r_1Q_1}, \quad \frac{Q_2P_2}{R_2Q_2}=\frac{Q_2p_2}{r_2Q_2}, \quad \frac{Q_3P_3}{R_3Q_3}=\frac{Q_3p_3}{r_3Q_3} \text{ etc.,}$$

but the denominators of the fractions on the right hand of the equations are all of them, by hypothesis, unity. Therefore the steepness of the curve at the points P_1, P_2, P_3 etc. is numerically represented by Q_1p_1, Q_2p_2, Q_3p_3, etc.

In our figure the points P_1, P_2, P_3 correspond to the

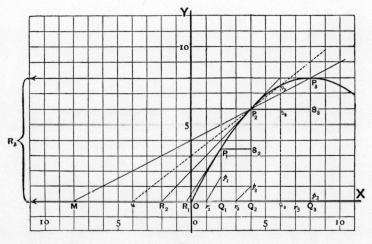

Fig. 4.

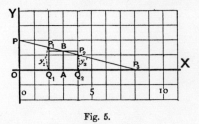

Fig. 5.

To face page 27.

values $x = 2$, $x = 4$, $x = 8$, and the lines Q_1p_1, Q_2p_2, Q_3p_3 are found on measurement to be $\frac{3}{2}$, 1, 0.

We may now tabulate the three degrees of steepness of the curve (or rates at which the function is increasing), corresponding to the three values of x :—

x	Steepness of curve = rate at which y is growing.
2	$\frac{3}{2}$
4	1
8	0

By the same method we may find as many more pairs of corresponding values as we choose, and it becomes obvious that the rate at which y or $f(x)$ is growing is itself a function of x (since it changes as x changes); and we may indicate this function by $f'(x)$. Then our table gives us pairs of corresponding values of x and $f'(x)$, and we may represent the connection between them by a curve, as usual. In this particular instance the curve turns out to be a straight line, and it is drawn out in Fig. 5.* Any vertical intercept on Fig. 5, therefore, represents the rate at which the vertical intercept for the same value of x on Fig. 4 is growing.

Thus we see that, given a curve of any variable and function, a simple graphical method enables us to find as many points as we like upon the curve of the same variable and a second function, which second function represents the rate at which the first function is growing; e.g., given a curve of time-and-height that tells us what the height of a body will be after the lapse of any given time, we can construct a curve of time-and-rate which will tell us at what rate that height is increasing, i.e. at what rate the body is rising, at any given time.

It remains for us to show that the common sense notion of the steepness of the curve at any point being measured by the steepness of the tangent is rigidly accurate. In proving this we shall throw further light on the conception of " rate

---

* Its formula is $y = 2 - \frac{x}{4}$.

of increase at a point " as applied to a movement, or other increase, which is constantly varying.

If I ask what is the average rate of increase of y between the points P_2 and P_3 (Fig. 4), I mean : If the increase of y bore a uniform ratio to the increase of x between the points P_2 and P_3, what would that ratio be ? or, if a point moved from P_2 to P_3 and if throughout its course its upward movement bore a uniform ratio to its forward movement, what would that ratio be ?   The answer obviously is $\dfrac{S_3P_3}{P_2S_3}$. Completing the figure as in Fig. 4 we have, by similar triangles, average ratio of increase of y to increase of x between the points P_2 and $P_3 = \dfrac{S_3P_3}{P_2S_3} = \dfrac{Q_3P_3}{MQ_3}$.

Now, keeping the same construction, we will let P_3 slip along the curve towards P_2, making the distance over which the average increase is to be taken smaller and smaller. Obviously as P_3 moves, Q_3, S_3, and M will move also, and the ratio $\dfrac{S_3P_3}{P_2S_3}$ will change its value, but the ratio $\dfrac{Q_3P_3}{MQ_3}$ will likewise change its value in precisely the same way, and will always remain equal to the other.   This is indicated by the dotted lines and the thin letters in Fig. 4.

Thus, however near P_3 comes to P_2 the average ratio of the increase of y to the increase of x between P_2 and P_3 will always be equal to $\dfrac{Q_3P_3}{MQ_3}$.   But this ratio, though it changes as P_3 approaches P_2, does not change indefinitely, or without limit ; on the contrary, it is always approaching a definite, fixed value, which it can never quite reach as long as P_3 remains distinct from P_2, but which it can approach within any fraction we choose to name, however small, if we make P_3 approach P_2 near enough.   It is easy to see what this ratio is.   For as P_3 approaches P_2, S_3 approaches P_2, Q_3 approaches Q_2, M approaches R_2, and therefore the ratio $\dfrac{Q_3P_3}{MQ_3}$ approaches the ratio $\dfrac{Q_2P_2}{R_2Q_2}$, which is the ratio that measures the steepness of the tangent at P_2.   We must realise exactly what is meant by this.   The lengths Q_2P_2 and R_2Q_2 have definite magnitudes, which do not change as P_3 approaches P_2, whereas the lengths S_3P_3 and $MR_2 + Q_2Q_3$, which distinguish Q_2P_2 and R_2Q_2 from Q_3P_3 and MQ_3 respectively, may be made as small as we please, and therefore as small fractions of the fixed lengths Q_2P_2 and R_2Q_2 as we please. Therefore the numerator and denominator of $\frac{Q_3P_3}{MQ_3}$ may be made to differ from the numerator and denominator of $\frac{Q_2P_2}{R_2Q_2}$ by *as small fractions of* Q_2P_2 *and* R_2Q_2 *themselves* as we please. That is to say, the former fraction, or ratio, may be made to approach the latter without limit. But the ratio $\frac{S_3P_3}{P_2S_3}$ is always the same as the ratio $\frac{Q_3P_3}{MQ_3}$, and therefore the ratio $\frac{S_3P_3}{P_2S_3}$ (or the average ratio of the increase of y to the increase of x between P_2 and P_3) may be made to approach the ratio $\frac{Q_2P_2}{R_2Q_2}$ without limit. Thus, though S_3P_3 and P_2S_3 can be made as small as we please absolutely, neither of them can be made as small as we please with reference to the other. On the contrary, they tend towards the fixed ratio $\frac{Q_2P_2}{R_2Q_2}$ as they severally approach zero. This is the limit of the average ratio of the increase of y to the increase of x between P_2 and P_3, and may be approached as nearly as we please by taking that average over a small enough part of the curve, that is by taking P_3 near enough to P_2. If we take the average over no space at all and make P_3 coincide with P_2, we may if we like say that the ratio of the increase of y to the increase of x *at* the point P_2 actually *is* $\frac{Q_2P_2}{R_2Q_2}$, or Q_2p_2 per unit. [*N.B.*—Let special note be taken of the conception of *rate per unit* as a limit to which a ratio approaches, as the related quantities diminish without limit.] But we must remember that since neither y nor x increases at all *at* a point, and since S_3P_3 and P_2S_3 both alike disappear when P_3 coincides with P_2, there is not really any ratio between them *at* the limit. But this is exactly in accordance with our original definition of the "rate of growth of y *at* a given point in its history" (p. 19), which we discovered to mean "the rate at which y would grow if all modifying circumstances ceased to operate," or "the limit of the average rate of growth of y between P_2 and P_3, as P_3 approaches P_2." As a matter of fact y never grows at that rate at all, for as soon as it grows ever so little it becomes subject to modifying influence.

We see, then, that as P_3 approaches P_2 the limiting position of the line P_3P_2M is P_2R_2, the tangent at P_2 (as indeed is evident to the eye), and the limiting ratio of the increase of y to the increase of x is $\dfrac{Q_2P_2}{R_2Q_2}$, or the steepness of the tangent at P_2. Thus "the steepness of the tangent at P_2" is the only exact interpretation we can give to "the steepness of the curve at P_2," and our common sense notion turns out to be rigidly scientific.

We see, then, that by drawing the tangents we can read $f'(x)$ as well as $f(x)$ from Fig. 4. But this is not easy. On the other hand, in Fig. 5, it is easy to read $f'(x)$, but not so easy to read $f(x)$. This latter may also be read, however. Let the student count the units of area included in the triangle OPP_3 (Fig. 5). He will find that they equal the units of length in Q_3P_3 (Fig. 4). Or if he take Q_2 in Fig. 5, corresponding to Q_2 in Fig. 4, he will find that the area OPP_2Q_2 (Fig. 5) contains as many units as the length Q_2P_2 (Fig. 4). Or again, taking Q_1 and Q_2, the area $Q_1P_1P_2Q_2$ (Fig. 5) contains as many units as the length S_2P_2 (Fig. 4), which gives the growth of y between P_1 and P_2.

Thus in Fig. 4 the absolute value of y, or $f(x)$, is indicated by *length* and the rate of growth of y, or $f'(x)$, by *slope* of the tangent; whereas in Fig. 5 $f'(x)$ is indicated by *length* and $f(x)$ by *area*. In either case the different character of the units in which $f(x)$ and $f'(x)$ are estimated indicates the difference in their nature, the one being *space* and the other *rate*.

The reason why the areas in Fig. 5 correspond to the lengths in Fig. 4 is not very difficult to understand, for we shall find that the units of length in S_2P_2 (Fig. 4), for example, and the units of area in $Q_1P_1P_2Q_2$ (Fig. 5) both represent exactly the same thing, viz. the product of the average rate of growth of y between P_1 and P_2 into the period over which that average growth is taken, which is obviously equivalent to the total actual growth of y between the two points.

To bring this out, let us call the average rate of growth of y, between P_1 and P_2, r, and the period over which that growth is taken, t. Then we shall have $rt =$ average rate of growth × period of growth = total growth.

Now, in Fig. 4, taking $OQ_1 = x_1$, $OQ_2 = x_2$, $Q_1P_1 = y_1$, $Q_2P_2 = y_2$, we shall have $r = \dfrac{P_2S_2}{P_1S_2} = \dfrac{y_2 - y_1}{x_2 - x_1}$, and $t = Q_1Q_2 = x_2 - x_1$, and $rt = \dfrac{y_2 - y_1}{x_2 - x_1}(x_2 - x_1) = y_2 - y_1 = P_2S_2$.

We must now find the representative of rt in Fig. 5, and to do so we must look for some line that represents r or $\dfrac{y_2 - y_1}{x_2 - x_1}$ or the average rate of growth of y between P_1 and P_2. Now the rate of growth of y at P_1 is represented by y'_1, and its rate of growth at P_2 by y'_2; and an inspection of the figure shows that it declines *uniformly* between the two points, so that the average rate will be half way between y'_1 and y'_2. This is represented by the line AB, which equals $\dfrac{Q_1P_1 + Q_2P_2}{2}$ or $\dfrac{y'_1 + y'_2}{2}$. We have then, in Fig. 5, $r = $ AB. But $t = x_2 - x_1$ or Q_1Q_2 as before. Therefore $rt = $ AB $\times Q_1Q_2$. Again, a glance at Fig. 5 will show that, by equality of triangles, the area AB $\times Q_1Q_2$ is equal to the area $Q_1P_1P_2Q_2$. Combining our results then, we have

$$Q_1P_1P_2Q_2 \text{ (Fig. 5)} = rt = P_2S_2 \text{ (Fig. 4)}$$

or units of length in $P_2S_2 = $ units of area in $Q_1P_1P_2Q_2$. Q.E.D.

Had the curve in Fig. 5 not been a straight line, the proof would have been the same in principle, though not so simple; and the areas would still have corresponded exactly to the lengths in the figure of the original function.*

It is essential that the reader should familiarise himself perfectly with the precise nature of the relation

---

* We have seen that the increment of y (or $y_2 - y_1$) equals the increment of x (or $x_2 - x_1$) multiplied by $\dfrac{y'_1 + y'_2}{2}$ $\left(\text{or } \dfrac{y_2 - y_1}{x_2 - x_1}\right)$.

Thus: increment of $y = $ increment of $x \times \dfrac{y'_1 + y'_2}{2}$; and $\dfrac{y'_1 + y'_2}{2} = \dfrac{f'(x_1) + f'(x_2)}{2}$; now the increment of y is the magnitude that differentiates y_2 from y_1, and is, therefore, called by Leibnitz the "quantitas differentialis" of y, though this term is only applied when y_1 and y_2 are taken very near together, so that the "quantitas differentialis" of y_1 and y_2 bears only a very small ratio to the "quantitas integralis," or integral magnitude of y_1 itself.

Thus when y_2 and x_2 approach y_1 and x_1 very nearly, we have subsisting between the two functions we have been investigating, and I make no apology, therefore, for dwelling on the subject at some length and even risking repetitions.

We have seen that $f'(x)$ is the rate at which $f(x)$ is increasing, or rate of growth of $f(x)$. And we measure the rate at which a function is increasing by the number of units which would be added to the function while one unit is being added to the variable if all the conditions which determine the relation should remain throughout the unit exactly what they were at its commencement.

Again, when we denote a certain function of x by the symbol $f(x)$, we have $y = f(x)$, and for $x = a$ $y = f(a)$, for $x = 1$ $y = f(1)$, for $x = 0$ $y = f(0)$, etc. This has been fully illustrated in previous tables (compare p. 24).

Thus if
$$f(x) = 128x - 16x^2,$$
then
$$f(2) = [128 \times 2 - 16 \times 2^2]$$
$$= 192.$$

In future, then, we may omit the intermediate stage and write at once $f(x) = 128x - 16x^2$; $f(2) = 192$, etc.

We may therefore epitomise the information given us by the curves in Figs. 1 and 3 (combined in Fig. 6) Thus—

differential of y_1 = differential of $x_1 \times \dfrac{f'(x_1)+f'(x_2)}{2}$, and as we approach the limit, and the difference between $f'(x_1)$ and $f'(x_2)$ becomes not only smaller itself, but a smaller fraction of $f'(x_1)$, we find that $\dfrac{f'(x_1)+f'(x_2)}{2}$ approaches $\dfrac{f'(x_1)+f'(x_1)}{2} = f'(x_1)$.

In the limit, then, we have differential of y_1 = differential of $x_1 \times f'(x_1)$; or generally, differential of y = differential of $x \times f'(x)$, where $f'(x)$ is *the coefficient which turns the differential of x into the differential of y*. Hence $f'(x)$ or y' is called the "differential coefficient" of $f(x)$ or y, and y or $f(x)$ is called the "integral" of $f'(x)$ or y'.

I insert this explanation in deference to the wish of a friend, who declares that he "can never properly understand a term scientifically until he understands it etymologically," and asks "why it is a coefficient and why it is differential." I believe his state of mind is typical.

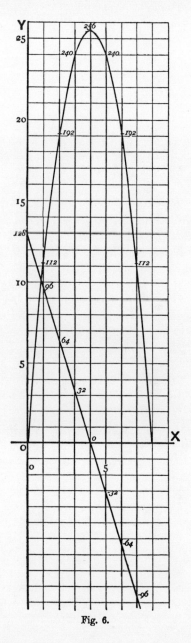

Fig. 6.

To face page 33.

$$f(x) = 128x - 16x^2 \qquad f'(x) = 128 - 32x$$

$f(0) = 0$	$f'(0) = 128$
$f(1) = 112$	$f'(1) = 96$
$f(2) = 192$	$f'(2) = 64$
$f(3) = 240$	$f'(3) = 32$
$f(4) = 256$	$f'(4) = 0$
$f(5) = 240$	$f'(5) = -32$
$f(6) = 192$	$f'(6) = -64$
$f(7) = 112$	$f'(7) = -96$
$f(8) = 0$	$f'(8) = -128$

which may be read in Fig. 6 from the lengths cut off by the two curves respectively on the vertical carried by the bearer as it passes points 0, 1, 2, 3, etc.

This table states the following facts :—At the commencement the height of the body [$f(x)$] is 0, but the rate at which that height is increasing [$f'(x)$] is 128 ft. per second. That is to say, the height would increase by 128 ft., while the time increased by one second, if the conditions which regulate the relations between the time that elapses and space traversed remained throughout the second exactly what they are at the beginning of it. But those conditions are continuously changing and never remain the same throughout any period of time, however small. At the end of the first second then, the height attained [$f(x)$] is, not 128 ft. as it would have been had there been no change of conditions, but 112 ft., and the rate at which that height is now growing is 96 ft. per second. That is to say, if the conditions which determine the relation between the time allowed and the space traversed were to remain throughout the second exactly what they are at the beginning of it, then the height of the body [$f(x)$] would *grow* 96 ft., while the time grew one second. Since these conditions change, however, the height grows, not 96 ft., but 80 ft. during the next second, so that after the lapse of two seconds it has reached the height of $(112 + 80) = 192$ ft., and is now *growing* at the rate of 64 ft. per second. After the lapse of four seconds the height of the body is 256 ft., and that height *is not growing at all.* That is to say, if the conditions remained exactly what they are at this moment, then the lapse of time would not affect the height of the body at all. But in this case we realise with peculiar vividness the fact that these conditions never do remain exactly what they are for any space of time, however brief. The movement of the body is the resultant of two tendencies, the constant tendency to *rise* 128 ft. per second in virtue of its initial velocity, and the growing tendency to *fall* in virtue of the continuous action of gravitation. At this moment these two tendencies are exactly equal, and *if they remained* equal then the body would rise 0 ft. per second, and the lapse of time would not affect its position. But of the two tendencies now exactly equal to each other, one is continuously increasing while the other remains constant. Therefore they will not remain equal during any period, however short. Up to this moment the body rises, after this moment the body falls. There is no period, however short, *during* which it is neither rising nor falling, but there is a point of time *at* which the conditions are such that if they were continued (which they are not) it *would* neither rise nor fall. This is expressed by saying that *at* that moment the rate at which the height is growing is 0. If the reader will pause to consider this special case, and then apply the like reasoning to other points in the history of the projectile, it may serve to fortify his conception of "rate." After 6 seconds the height is 192, and the rate at which it is growing is − 64 ft.-per-second. That is to say, the body is *falling* at the rate of 64 ft.-per-second. At the end of 8 seconds the height is 0, and the rate at which the height is growing is − 128 ft.-per-second.

All this is represented on the table, which may be continued indefinitely on the supposition that the body is free to fall below the point from which it was originally projected.

The instance of the vertically projected body must be kept for permanent reference in the reader's mind, so that if any doubt or confusion as to the relation between $f'(x)$ and $f(x)$ should occur, he may be able to use it as a tuning fork : $f'(x)$ is the rate at which $f(x)$ is growing, so that if $f(x)$ is the space traversed, then $f'(x)$ is the rate of motion, *i.e.* the rate at which the space traversed, $f(x)$, is being increased.

Now, when we are regarding time solely as a regulator of the height of the body, we may without any great stretch of language speak of the *effect* of the lapse of time in allowing or securing a definite result in height. Thus the effect of 1 second would be represented by 112 ft., the effect of 4 seconds by 256 ft., the effect of 7 seconds by 112 ft., the effect of 8 seconds by 0 ft. And to make it clear that we mean to register only the net result of the whole lapse of time in question, we might call this the "total effect" of so many seconds. In this case $f(x)$ will represent the total effect of the lapse of x seconds, regarded as a condition affecting the height of the body. What, then, will $f'(x)$ signify? It will signify, as always, the rate at which $f(x)$ is increasing. That is to say, it will signify the rate at which additions to the time are at this point increasing the effect, *i.e.* the rate at which the effect is growing. Now, since more time must always be added on at the margin of the time that has already elapsed, we may say that $f(x)$ represents the *total effect* of x seconds of time in giving height to the body, and that $f'(x)$ represents the *effectiveness* of time, added at the margin of x seconds, in *increasing* the height. Or, briefly, $f(x) =$ total effect, $f'(x) =$ marginal effectiveness.

Here the change of terms from "effect" to "effectiveness" may serve to remind us that in the two cases we are dealing with two different kinds of magnitude— in the one case *space* measured in feet absolutely (effect), in the other case *rate* measured in feet-per-second.

Before passing on to the economic interpretation of all that has been said, we will deal very briefly with another scientific illustration, which may serve as a transition.

Suppose we have a carbon furnace in which the carbon burns at a temperature of 1500° centigrade, and suppose we are using it to heat a mass of air under

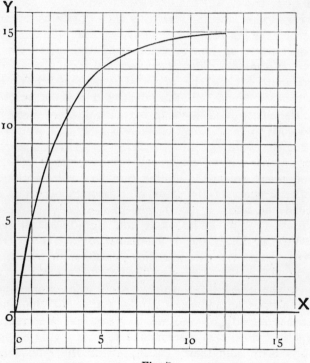

Fig. 7.

given conditions. Obviously the temperature to which we raise the air will be a function of the amount of carbon we burn, and will be a function which will increase as the variable increases ; but not without limit, for it can never exceed the temperature of 1500°. Suppose the conditions are such that the first pound

of carbon burnt raises the temperature of the air from
0° to 500°, *i.e.* raises it one-third of the way from its
present temperature to that of the burning carbon, then
(neglecting certain corrections) the second pound of
carbon burnt will again raise the temperature one-third
of the way from its present point (500°) to that of
the carbon (1500°). That is to say, it will raise it to
833·3°; and so forth. Measuring the pounds of carbon
consumed along the axis of x and the degrees centigrade to which the air is raised along the axis of y
(100° to a unit), we may now represent the connection between $f(x)$ and x by a curve.* Its general
form may be seen in Fig. 7, and we shall have the
total effect of the carbon in raising the temperature
represented by $f(x)$, and assuming the following values :—

$$f(0) = \ 0 \qquad\qquad f(4) = 12\text{·}04 \qquad f(8) = 14\text{·}42$$
$$f(1) = \ 5\,[\,= 500°] \quad f(5) = 13\text{·}02 \qquad f(9) = 14\text{·}61$$
$$f(2) = \ 8\text{·}3 \qquad\qquad f(6) = 13\text{·}68 \qquad f(10) = 14\text{·}74$$
$$f(3) = 10\text{·}5 \qquad\quad f(7) = 14\text{·}12 \qquad f(11) = 14\text{·}83$$
$$f(12) = 14\text{·}88$$

Now here, as before, we may proceed (either graphically, see p. 26, or by aid of the rules of the calculus)
to construct a second curve, the curve of x and $f'(x)$,
which shall set forth the connection between x and the
steepness of the first curve, *i.e.* the connection between
the value of x and the rate at which $f(x)$ is growing.†
Again allowing 100° to the unit, measured on the axis
of y, we shall obtain (Fig. 8)—

$$f'(0) = 6\text{·}08 \qquad f'(4) = 1\text{·}2 \qquad f'(8) = \text{·}24$$
$$f'(1) = 4\text{·}05 \qquad f'(5) = \ \text{·}8 \qquad f'(9) = \text{·}16$$
$$f'(2) = 2\text{·}7 \qquad\ f'(6) = \ \text{·}53 \qquad f'(10) = \text{·}1$$
$$f'(3) = 1\text{·}8 \qquad\ f'(7) = \ \text{·}35 \qquad \text{etc.}$$

What then will $f'(x)$ represent? **Here as always**

---

* The formula will be $y = f(x) = 15 \left\{ 1 - \left(\tfrac{2}{3} \right)^{x} \right\}$

† Its formula will be $15 \left(\tfrac{2}{3} \right)^{x} \log_{e} \left(\tfrac{3}{2} \right)$.

we have $f'(x) =$ the rate at which $f(x)$ is growing. But $f(x) =$ the heat to which the air is raised, *i.e.* the total effect of the carbon. Therefore $f'(x)$ is the rate at which carbon, added at the margin, will increase the heat, or the marginal effectiveness of carbon in raising the heat. We have $x =$ quantity of carbon burnt, $f(x) =$ total effect of x in raising the heat of the air, $f'(x) =$ marginal effectiveness of additions to x.

Comparing the illustration of the heated air with

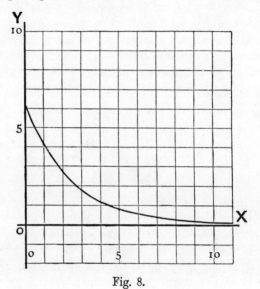

Fig. 8.

that of the falling body we find that pounds of carbon have taken the place of seconds of time as the variable, total rise of temperature has taken the place of total space traversed as the first function of the variable, rate at which additions to carbon are increasing the temperature has taken the place of rate at which additions to the time allowed are increasing the space traversed, as the derived function; but in both cases the derived function represents the rate at which the first function is growing, in both cases the first function represents

the total efficiency of any given quantity of the variable,
and the derived function represents its effectiveness at
any selected margin, so that in both cases the relation
of $f'(x)$ to $f(x)$ is identical.

And now at last we may return to the economic
interpretation of the curves.

Assuming that Fig. 1 (p. 9) represents the connection
between some economic function and its variable, as, for
example, the connection between the quantity of coal I
burn and the sum of advantages or gratifications I
derive from it, and assuming further that one unit along
the axis of x is taken to mean one ton of coal per month,
we shall have no difficulty in reading Fig. 1 as follows :
$f(0) = 0$, *i.e.* if I burn no coal I get no benefit from
burning it ; $f(1) = 11\cdot2$, *i.e.* the total effect of burning
one ton of coal per month is represented by $11\cdot2$ units
of satisfaction ; $f(2) = 19\cdot2$, *i.e.* the total effect of burning two tons of coal a month is greater than that of
burning one ton a month, but not twice as great.   The
difference to my comfort between burning no coal and
burning a ton a month is greater than the difference
between burning one and burning two tons.   So again,
$f(4) = 25\cdot6$, *i.e.* the total effect of four tons of coal per
month in adding to my comfort is represented by $25\cdot6$
units of gratification, and at this point its total effect is
at its maximum ; for now I have as much coal as I
want, and if I were forced to burn more the total effect
of that greater quantity would be less than that of a
smaller quantity, or $f(5)$ is less than $f(4)$.   At last the
point would arrive at which if I were forced to choose between burning, say, eight tons of coal a month and burning
none at all, I should be quite indifferent in the matter.
The total effect of eight tons of coal per month as a
direct instrument of comfort would then be nothing.
And if more yet were forced upon me at last I should
prefer the risk of dying of cold to the certainty of
being burned to death, and $f(x)$ would be a negative
quantity.

It must be observed that I am not here speaking of the *construction* of economic curves, but of their *interpretation* supposing we had them (see p. 15). But it will be seen presently that the construction of such curves is quite conceivable ideally, and that there is no absurdity involved in speaking of so many units of gratification. It is extremely improbable, however, that any actual economic curve would coincide with that of Fig. 1 (see p. 48).

Such would be the interpretation of Fig. 1, $f(x)$ being read as the curve of quantity-and-total-effect of coal as a producer of comfort under given conditions of consumption. What then would be the interpretation of Fig. 3 or $f'(x)$? Obviously $f'(x)$, signifying the rate of growth of $f(x)$, or the ratio of the increase of $f(x)$ to the increase of x at any point, would mean the rate at which an additional supply of coal is increasing my comfort, or the marginal effectiveness of coal as a producer of comfort to me. This marginal effectiveness of course varies with the amount I already enjoy. That is to say, $f'(x)$ assumes different values as x changes. When I have no coal, the marginal effectiveness is very high. That is to say, increments of coal would add to my comfort at a great rate, $f'(0) = 12 \cdot 8$. When I already command a ton a month further increments of coal would add to my comfort at a less rapid rate, $f'(1) = 9 \cdot 6$; when I have four tons a month further increments would not add to my comfort at all, $f'(4) = 0$, after that yet further increments would detract from my comfort, $f'(5) = -32$.

In thus interpreting Figs. 1 and 3 we have substituted consumption of coal per month (measured in tons), for lapse of time (measured in seconds), as our variable ; sum of advantages derived from consuming the coal, for space traversed by the projectile, as $f(x)$, or the total effect of the variable ; and rate per unit at which coal is increasing comfort, for rate per unit at which time is increasing the space traversed, as $f'(x)$, or the marginal effectiveness of the variable.

If we call $f(x)$ the "total utility" of x tons of coal per month, we might call $f'(x)$ the "marginal usefulness" of coal when the supply is x tons per month.

The reader should now turn back to p. 33, and read the table of successive values of $f(x)$ and $f'(x)$ with the subsequent comments and interpretations, substituting the economic meanings of x, $f(x)$, and $f'(x)$ for the physical ones throughout.

A similar re-reading of Figs. 7 and 8 will also be instructive.

Before going on to the further consideration of the total effect and marginal effectiveness of a commodity as functions of the quantity possessed, it will be well to point out a method of reading $f'(x)$ which will bring it more nearly within the range of our ordinary experiences, and make it stand for something more definitely realisable by the practical intellect than can be the case with the abstract idea of rate.

Reverting to our first interpretation of Fig. 3, we remember that $f'(2) = 64$ means that after the lapse of 2 seconds the body will be rising *at the rate* of 64 ft. per second ; but it is entirely untrue that it will actually rise 64 ft. during the next following second. We see by Fig. 1 that it will only rise 48 ft. in that second. This is because the rate, which was 64 ft. per second at the beginning of the second, has constantly changed during the lapse of the second itself. But the rate of 64 ft. per second is the same thing as the rate of 6 4 ft. per tenth of a second (or per ·1 second), and this again is the same as the rate ·64 ft. per ·01 second, or ·000064 ft. per ·000001 second, and I may therefore read Fig. 3 thus : $f'(2) = 64$, *i.e.* after the lapse of 2 seconds the body will be rising at the rate of 64 millionths of a foot per millionth of a second. Now, we should have to allow many millionths of a second to elapse before the rate of movement materially altered, and therefore we may with a very close approximation to the truth say that the rate of motion will

be the same at the end as it was at the beginning
of the first millionth of a second, *i.e.* 64 millionths
of a foot per millionth of a second.   Hence it will
be approximately true to say that during the next
millionth of a second the body will actually rise 64
millionths of a foot (compare p. 20).*   But a rise of
64 millionths of a foot would be a concrete *effect ; hence
if we translate the* EFFECTIVENESS *of the variable into terms
of a small enough unit, it tells us within any degree of
accuracy we may demand the actual* EFFECT *of the next small
increment of the variable.*   This is expressed by saying
that " in the limit " each small increment actually produces this effect ; which means that by making the
increments small enough we may make the proposition
as nearly true as we like.

Thus [assuming the ordinary formula $y = 16x^2$ to
be absolutely correct] it is nearly true to say that when
a body has been falling 2 seconds it will fall 64
millionths of a foot in the next millionth of a second,
128 millionths of a foot in the next 2 millionths of a
second, $64n$ millionths of a foot in the next n millionths of a second, so long as n is an insignificant
number in comparison to one million.   What is nearly
true when the unit is small and more and more nearly
true as the unit grows smaller is said to be " true in
the limit, as the unit decreases."

Marginal *effectiveness* of the variable, then, may always
be read as marginal *effect* per unit of very small units
of increment.   And in this sense we shall generally
understand it.   Total effect and unitary marginal effect
will then be magnitudes of the same nature or character ;
and indeed the unitary marginal effect will itself
be a total effect in a certain sense, the total effect
namely of one small unit, added at that particular place.
Even when we are not dealing with small units we

* It would be [assuming the formula to be absolutely true]
63·999984 millionths of a foot.   The error, therefore, would be
$\frac{16}{1000000}$ or $\frac{1}{62500}$ in 64.

may still speak of the marginal effect of a unit of the commodity, but in that case the effect of a unit of the commodity at the margin of x will no longer correspond closely to the marginal effectiveness of the commodity at x. It will correspond to the *average* marginal effectiveness of the commodity between x, at which its application begins, and $x + 1$, at which it ends. And if the effect of the next unit after the ath is z, it will probably not be true (as it is in the case of small units) that the effect of the next two units will be nearly $2z$. A reference to Figs. 1, 3, 7, 8, and a comparison of the last column and the last but one in the table of p. 4, will sufficiently illustrate this point; and the economic illustration of the next paragraph will furnish an instance of the correspondence, in the limit, between the effectiveness of the commodity and the effect of a small unit.

Reverting to Figs. 4 and 5 (p. 25) we have Q_1p_1 in Fig. 4 $= Q_1P_1$ in Fig. 5. But we have seen that if we start from P_1 in Fig. 4 and move a very little way along the curve, the ratio of the increment of x to the increment of y will be very nearly $\frac{r_1Q_1}{Q_1p_1}$; or in the limit $\frac{\text{increment of } x}{\text{increment of } y} = \frac{r_1Q_1}{Q_1p_1}$. But $r_1Q_1 = 1$, therefore in the limit $\frac{\text{increment of } x}{\text{increment of } y} = \frac{1}{Qp_1}$ (Fig. 4) $= \frac{1}{Q_1P_1}$ (Fig. 5), or, in the limit, $Q_1P_1 \times$ increment of $x =$ increment of y. Now in Fig. 5 increments of x are measured along OX, and therefore (if we follow the ordinary system of interpretation) we shall regard $Q_1P_1 \times$ increment of x, as an area, and it will be seen that as x decreases the area in question approximates to a thin slice cut vertically from the triangle $Q_1P_1P_3$. But we have seen that areas cut in vertical slices out of this triangle correspond to lengths in Fig. 4, or portions of the total effect of the variable. Thus if a small unit is taken, the *effect* of units of a commodity applied at any margin (Fig. 4) is approximately represented by the *effectiveness* of the commodity at that margin (Fig. 5) multiplied by the number of units. And in the limit this relation is said to hold absolutely (compare pp. 21, 42).

The method of reading curves of quantity-and-marginal-effectiveness as though they were curves of quantity-and-marginal-effect may be illustrated by the following example.

Fig. 9 represents part of the curve of quantity-and-marginal-effectiveness of wheat in Great Britain, based upon a celebrated estimate made about the beginning of the eighteenth century.* In the figure the unit of x is (roughly speaking) about 20 millions of bushels; and if

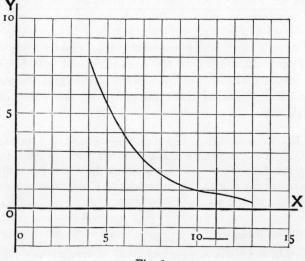

Fig. 9.

we place our quantity-index eleven units from the origin, that will mean that we suppose the supply of wheat in Great Britain to be 220 millions of bushels per annum. Our curve asserts that when we have that supply additions of wheat will have an " effectiveness " in supplying our wants represented by ·8 per 20 million bushels; but we cannot translate the " effectiveness " into the actual " effect " which 20 millions of bushels

* The estimate is generally known as "Gregory King's," and its formula is

$$60y = 1500 - 374x + 33x^2 - x^3.$$

would have ; because the "effectiveness" would not continue the same if so large an addition were made to our
supply. On the contrary it would drop from ·8 to ·6.
But ·8 per 20,000,000 bushels is ·00000008 per 2
bushels and ·00000004 per bushel, and since the addition of another bushel to the 220 millions already
possessed will not materially affect the usefulness or
effectiveness of wheat at the margin, we may say that
that effectiveness remains constant during the consumption of the bushel of wheat, and therefore, given
a supply of 20,000,000 bushels a year, not only is the
"marginal effectiveness" of wheat ·8 per 20,000,000
bushels or ·0000004 per bushel, but the "marginal
effect" of a bushel is ·00000004.   Thus, if we had two
commodities, W and V, and curves of their quantity-and-
marginal-usefulness or effectiveness similar to that in
Fig. 9, the vertical intercepts on the quantity-indices
would indicate the marginal usefulness per unit of the
two commodities, and if we then selected "small" units
of each commodity bearing in each case the same proportion (say $1 : z$) to the unit to which the curve of the
commodity was drawn, we should then have the marginal
utility or effect of the small units of the two commodities
proportional to the length of the vertical intercepts, and
calling the small unit of W, w, and the small unit of V, v,
and the ratio of the marginal usefulness of W to that of V,
r, we should have

marginal utility of $w = r$ × marginal utility of v

„   „ $2w = 2r$ × marginal utility of v.

etc.   etc. (compare p. 56)

We shall make it a convention henceforth to use
Roman capitals A, X, W, etc., to signify commodities,
italic minuscules a, x, w, etc., to signify units of these
commodities (generally "small" units in the sense explained), and italic capitals, A, B, etc., to signify persons.
Thus we shall speak of the marginal *usefulness* or *effectiveness* of A, W, etc., and the marginal *utility* or *effect* of
a, w, etc.

What precise interpretation we are to give to our "units of satisfaction" or "utility" measured on the axis of y is another matter, the consideration of which must be reserved for a later stage of our inquiry (see pp. 52, 78).

Jevons uses the terms "total utility" and "final degree of utility," meaning by the latter what I have termed "marginal usefulness" or "marginal effectiveness." His terminology hardly admits of sufficient distinction between "marginal effectiveness," *i.e.* the *rate* per unit at which the commodity is satisfying desire, and the "marginal effect" of a unit of the commodity, *i.e.* the actual result which it produces when applied at the margin. I think this has sometimes confused his readers, and I hope that my attempt to preserve the distinction will not be found vexatious. Note that the curves are always curves of quantity-and-marginal-usefulness, but that we can read them with more or less accuracy according to the smallness of the supposed increment into curves of quantity-and-marginal-utility for small increments.

If the reader has now gained a precise idea of the total utility or effect and the marginal usefulness of commodities, he will see without difficulty that when we take a broad general view of life we are chiefly concerned with those commodities the total utility of which (or their total effect in securing comfort, giving pleasure, averting suffering, etc.) is high. In considering from a general point of view our own material welfare or that of a nation, our first inquiries will concern the necessaries of life, food, water, clothing, shelter, fuel. For these are the things a moderate supply of which has the highest total utility. The sum of advantages we derive from them collectively is, indeed, no other than the advantage of the life they support. This is what economists have in view when they speak of the "value in use" of such a commodity as water, and say that nothing is more "useful" than it. They mean that the total advantage derived from

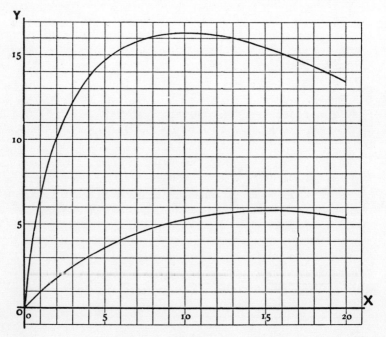

Fig. 10.

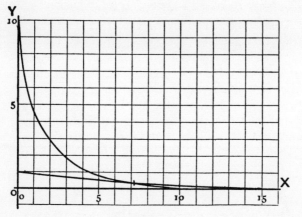

Fig. 11.

To face page 47.

even a small supply of water, the total difference
between a little water and no water, is enormously
great. The graphical expression of this would be a
curve (connecting the total utility of water with its
quantity) which would rise rapidly and to a great height.

But if it is obvious that when we look upon life as
a whole, and in the abstract, we are chiefly concerned
with total utilities, and ask what are the commodities
we could least afford to dispense with altogether, it is
equally obvious that in detail and in concrete practice
we are chiefly concerned not with the total utility but
the marginal usefulness of things, or rather, their marginal utility ; and we ask, not what is my whole stock
of such a commodity worth to me, but how much would
a little *more* of it *add* to my satisfaction or a little less
of it detract therefrom. For instance, we do not ask,
What is the total advantage I derive from all the water
I can command, but what additional advantage should I
derive from the extra supply of water for a bath-room,
or for a garden hose ? Materfamilias does not ask
what advantage she derives from having a kitchen fire,
but she asks, what additional advantage she would
derive by keeping up her kitchen fire after dinner, by
heating the oven every day, or by always letting the
girls have a fire in the room when they are " practising."
Or inversely, we do not ask what disadvantage we
should incur by ceasing to burn coal, but what disadvantage we should incur by letting our fires go down
earlier in the day, or having fewer of them. And note
that this inquiry as to marginal usefulness of a commodity is made on its own merits, and wholly without
reference to the total utilities of the articles in question.
The fact that I should be much worse off without
clothes than without books does not make me spend
fifteen shillings on a new waistcoat instead of on
Rossetti's works, if I think that the latter will *add* more
to my comfort and enjoyment than the former. For
f (clothes) may be as much bigger than ϕ (books) as it

likes, but if f' (clothes) is smaller than ϕ' (books) I shall spend the money on the books. So much is this the case that we habitually lose sight of the connection between ϕ' (books) and ϕ (books), between f' (clothes) and f (clothes), and do not think, for instance, of ϕ' (books) as marking the rate at which additional books increase the gratification *we derive from books*, but simply as marking the rate at which they increase our gratification in general.

Before developing certain consequences of the principles we have been examining, let us try to get a better representation of our supposed economic functions than is supplied by the diagram of a projected body. It will be remembered that we saw reason to think that a large class of economic functions, representing total utilities, would bear an analogy to our Fig. 1 in so far as they would first increase and then decrease as the variable (*i.e.* the supply of the commodity) increased. But it is highly improbable that any economic curve would increase and decrease in the symmetrical manner there represented. It is not likely, for instance, that the inconvenience of having a unit too much of a commodity would be exactly equivalent to the inconvenience of having a unit too little. As a rule it would be decidedly less. Our economic functions, then, will, in many instances, rise more rapidly than they fall. The connection of such a function and its variable is represented by the upper curve on Fig. 10,* which rises rapidly at first, then rises slowly, and then falls more slowly still. Household linen might give a curve something of this character. It is not exactly a necessary of life, but the sum of advantages conferred by even a small stock is great. The rate at which additions to the stock add to its total

* The conditions stated in the text will be complied with by a function of the form $a \log_e (x+b) - \log b - x$; and there are some theoretical reasons for thinking that such a function may be a fair approximation to some classes of actual economic functions. The upper curve in Fig. 9 is drawn to the formula $y = 11 \log_e (x+1) - x$.

utility is at first rapid, but it declines pretty quickly. At last we should have as much as we wanted and should find it positively inconvenient to stow away any more. The excess, however, would have to be very great indeed in order to reduce us to a condition as deplorable as if we had no linen at all. By way of practice in interpreting economic curves, let us suppose the unit of household linen, measured along the base line, to be such an amount as might be purchased for £3. The curve would then represent the following case, which might well be that of a young housekeeper with a four or five roomed cottage, and not much space for storage : Household linen (sheets, tablecloths, towels, etc.) to the amount of some £6 or £10 worth ($x = 2$ or $3\frac{1}{3}$) is little short of a necessity. After this additions to the stock, though very acceptable, are not so urgently needed, and when the stock has reached £18 or £20 worth ($x = 6$ or $6\frac{2}{3}$) our housekeeper will consider herself very well supplied, and will scarcely desire more. Still, if she could get it for nothing, she would be glad to find room for it up to, say, £30 worth ($x = 10$). If after this any one should offer her a present of more she would prefer to find a polite excuse for not accepting it, but would not be much troubled if she had to take it, unless the amount were very large ;* but when the total stock had reached, say, £45 ($x = 15$), the inconvenience would become serious, and our heroine, on the whole, would be nearly as hard put to it by having £15 worth too much as she would have been by having £12 worth too little. If her stock were still increased till it reached £60 worth ($x = 20$) she would be as badly off as if she had only £11 : 8s. worth ($x = 3\frac{4}{5}$). At this point our "epic of the hearth" breaks off.

We may, of course, apply to this curve the process with which we are already familiar, and may find the derived function which represents the marginal effectiveness or

---

* We are supposing throughout that the conditions exclude sale or barter of the unvalued part of the stock.

usefulness of linen, that is to say, the rate at which
increments of linen are increasing the sum of advantages derived from it.   This marginal effectiveness or
usefulness of linen is set forth on the higher curve in
Fig. 11;* on which may be read the facts already
elaborated in connection with the curve on Fig. 10,
the only difference being that the specific increase
between any values of x is more easily read on Fig. 10,
and the *rate* of increase at any point more easily read
on Fig. 11.

An analogous pair of curves, with other constants,†
may be found in the lower lines in Figs. 10 and 11.‡
They might represent respectively the total utility and
the marginal usefulness of china, for example.   In Fig. 10
the lower curve does not rise so rapidly or so high as
the other.   That is to say, we suppose the total advantage derived from as much china as one would care to
have to be far less than that derived from a similarly
full supply of household linen.   To be totally deprived
of china (not including coarse crockery in the term)
would be a less privation than to be totally deprived
of linen.   But we also observe that at a certain point,
when the curve of linen is rising very slowly, the curve
of china is rising rather more rapidly.   That is to say,
if our supplies of both linen and china increase *pari
passu*, unit for unit (£3 worth is the unit we have supposed), then there comes a point at which increments of
china would add to our enjoyment at a greater rate than
similar increments of linen, although in the mass the
linen has done much more to make us comfortable than
the china.

On the curves of Fig. 11 this point is indicated by
the point at which the curve of the marginal usefulness

* Its formula is $\frac{11}{x+1} - 1$.

† See p. 9.

‡ They are drawn to the formulæ $y = 30 \log_e (x+15) - \log_e 15 - x$
and $y = \frac{30}{x+15} - 1$ respectively.

of china crosses, and thenceforth runs above, the curve
of the marginal usefulness of linen.

Now if I possess a certain stock of linen and a
certain stock of china, and am in doubt as to the
use to make of an opportunity which presents itself
for adding in certain proportions to either or both,
how will the problem present itself to me? I shall
not concern myself at all with the total utilities,
but shall simply ask, "Will the quantity of linen or the
quantity of china I can now secure *add* most to my
satisfaction." The total gratification I derive from the
two articles together is made up of their two total utilities
(represented by two straight lines, viz. the vertical intercepts made by the two curves on Fig. 10), and it is
indifferent to me whether I increase the one already
greatest or the other, as long as the increase is the
the same. I therefore ask not which curve is the *highest*,
but which is the *steepest* at the points I have reached on
them respectively, or since the curves on Fig. 11 represent the steepness of those on Fig. 10, I ask which of
these is highest. In other words, I examine the $f'(x)$'s,
not the $f(x)$'s; I compare the marginal usefulness and
not the total utilities of the two commodities. If
the choice is between one small unit of china and one
similar unit of linen, I shall ask "Which of the two has
the higher marginal utility." If my stock of both is
low, the answer will be "linen." If my stock of both is
high, it will be "china." If, on the other hand, the
choice is between one small unit of china and *two* similar
units of linen, the question will be "Is the marginal
effectiveness of china *twice* as great as that of linen," if
not I shall choose the linen, since double the amount at
anything more than half the effectiveness gives a balance
of effect over what the other alternative would yield.
If it seems difficult to imagine the mental process by
which one thing shall be pronounced exactly *twice* as
useful as another, we may express the same thing in
other terms by asking whether half a small unit of china

is as useful to us (or is worth as much to us) as one small unit of linen, thus transferring the inequality from the utilities to the quantities, and the equality from the quantities to the utilities.*

Such considerations as these spontaneously solve the problem that suggested itself at the threshold of our inquiries (p. 15) as to the theoretical possibility of fixing a unit of utility or satisfaction, and so theoretically constructing economic curves. We now see clearly enough that though our psychological arithmetic is so little developed that the simplest sums in hedonistic multiplication or division seem impossible and even absurd, yet, as a matter of fact, we are constantly comparing and weighing against each other the most heterogeneous satisfactions and determining which is the greater. The enjoyment of fresh air and friendship, of fresh eggs and opportunities of study, all in definite quantities, are weighed against each other when we canvass the advantages of residence in London within reach of our friends and the British Museum and residence in the country with fresh air and fresh eggs. Nay, we may even regard space and time as commodities each with its varying marginal usefulness. This year I eagerly accept a present of books which will occupy a great deal of space in my house, but will save me an occasional journey to the library; for the marginal usefulness of my space and of my time are such that I find an advantage in losing space and gaining time under given conditions of exchange. Next year my space is more contracted, and its marginal usefulness is therefore higher; so I decline a similar present, preferring the occasional loss of half an hour to the permanent cramping of my movements in my own study.

Thus we see that the most absolutely heterogeneous

* Observe that this transfer can only be made in the case of *small* units, for it assumes that half a unit of china is half as useful as a whole unit, which implies that the marginal usefulness of china remains the same throughout the unit.

satisfactions are capable of being practically equated against one another, and therefore may be regarded as theoretically *reducible to a common measure*, and consequently capable of being measured off in lengths, and connected by a curve with the lengths representing the quantities of commodity to which they correspond. We might, for instance, take the effort of doing a given amount of work as the standard unit by which to estimate the magnitude of satisfaction. Hence the truth of the remark, "Pleasures cannot be measured in feet, and they cannot be measured in pounds; but they can be measured in foot-pounds" (Launhardt). If I only had one ton of coal per month, how much lifting work should I be willing to do for a hundredweight of coal? If I had two tons a month, how much lifting work would I then do for a hundredweight? Definite answers to these two questions and other similar ones are conceivable; and they would furnish material for a curve on which the utility of one, two, three, etc. hundredweight of coal per month would be estimated in foot-pounds. In academical circles it is not unusual to take an hour of correcting examination papers as the standard measure of pleasures and pains. A pleasure to secure which a man would be willing to correct examination papers for six hours (choosing his time and not necessarily working continuously) must be regarded as six times as great as one for which he would only correct papers for an hour. If we wished to reduce satisfactions so estimated to the foot-pound standard, we should only have to ascertain in the case of each of the university dignitaries in question how many foot-pounds of heaving work he would undertake in order to escape an hour's work at the examination mill. Obviously this change of measure would not affect the *relative* magnitudes of the satisfactions already estimated on the other scale. It does not, then, matter what we suppose the standard unit of satisfaction to be, provided we retain it unchanged throughout any set of investigations.

It should be noted that to be theoretically accurate we must not suppose the quantity of work offered for the same quantity of the commodity to change over different parts of the curve, but rather the quantity of the commodity for which the same fixed quantity of work is offered. For if we change the quantity of work, we thereby generally change its hedonistic value per unit also, inasmuch as 400 foot-tons of work, for instance, would generally be more than twice as irksome as 200 foot-tons.

In working out an imaginary example, however, we will ignore this fact, and will suppose the hedonistic value of 100 foot-tons to be constant. Let us, then, suppose that a house-holder would be willing to do 3300 foot-tons of work* for a certain amount of linen, if he could not get it any other way. We will reckon that amount of linen the unit, and calling x the amount of linen and y its total utility, we shall have for $x = 1$ $y = 3300$, or allowing 500 foot-tons to the unit of y, $x = 1$ $y = 6\cdot6$. Now suppose that having secured one unit, our householder would be willing to do 1750 foot-tons of work for a second unit, but not more. This would be represented on our scale by $3\cdot5$, which, added to the previous $6\cdot6$, would give $y = 10\cdot1$ for $x = 2$. For yet another unit of linen, perhaps no more than 1125 foot-tons would be offered, represented by $2\cdot2$ on our scale, or $y = 12\cdot3$ for $x = 3$, etc. On comparing these suppositions with Fig. 10 (p. 47), it will be found that this case would be graphically represented by the upper curve of that figure. It will be seen that though we have imagined an ideally perfect and exact power of estimating what one would be willing to do under given circumstances in order to secure a certain object of desire, yet there is nothing theoretically absurd in the imaginary process; so that the construction of economic curves may henceforth be regarded as theoretically possible.

The reader may find it interesting to attempt to construct the economic curves that depict the history of some of his own wants. Taking some such article as coffee or tobacco, let him ask himself how much work he would do for a single cup or pipe per week or per day sooner than go entirely

---

* An ordinary day's work is reckoned at 300 foot-tons; a dock labourer does 325 (Mulhall).

without, how much for a second, etc., and dotting down
the results, see whether they seem to follow any law and
form any regular curve.   If they do not, it probably shows
that his imagination is not sufficiently vivid and accurate to
enable him to realise approximately what he would be willing
to do under varying circumstances.   In any case he will
probably soon convince himself of the perfect theoretical
legitimacy of thus supposing actual concrete economic curves
to be constructed.   But even if he cannot tell what amount
of work he would be willing to do under the varying circumstances, obviously *there is* a given amount, which, as a matter
of fact, he would be willing to do under any given circumstances.   Thus the curve *really exists*, whether he is able to
trace it or not.

We may now return to our curves with a clear conscience, knowing that for any object of desire at any
moment there actually exists a curve (could we but get
at it) representing the complete history of the varying
total utility that would accompany the varying quantity
possessed.   The man who knows most nearly what that
curve is, in each case, has the most powerful and
accurate economic imagination, and is best able to pre-
dict what his expenditure, habits of work, etc. would
be under changed circumstances.

We have now actually constructed some hypothetical
curves (pp. 48, 50), and have shown that there are certain properties, easy to represent, which a large class of
economic curves must have (pp. 15, 48) ; and we have
further shown that we are practically engaged, from
day to day, in considering and comparing the marginal
utilities of units of heterogeneous articles, that is to say,
in constructing and comparing fragments of economic
curves.

We have seen, too, that if I had a chance of getting
more china or more linen I should not consider the total
utilities of these commodities, but the marginal utilities
of the respective quantities between which the option
lay.

And so, too, if I had the opportunity of exchanging a given quantity of china for a given quantity of linen, or the reverse, I should consider the marginal utilities of those quantities. Thus we see that the *equivalence in worth* to me of units of two commodities is measured by their marginal, not their total, utilities, and in the limit (p. 44) is directly proportional to their marginal effectiveness or usefulness. If, for the stocks I possess, the marginal usefulness of linen is twice as great as that of china, *i.e.* if f' (linen) $= 2\phi'$ (china), then I shall be glad to sacrifice small units of china in order to secure similar units of linen at anything up to the rate of two to one. But this very process, by decreasing my stock of china and increasing my stock of linen, will depress the marginal usefulness of the latter and increase that of the former, so that now we have

$$f' \text{ (linen)} < 2\phi' \text{ (china)}.$$

If, however,

$$f' \text{ (linen)} > \phi' \text{ (china)}$$

is still true, I shall still wish to sacrifice china for the sake of linen, unit for unit, until by the action of the same principle we have reached the point at which we have

$$f' \text{ (linen)} = \phi'(\text{china}).$$

After this I shall not be willing to sacrifice china for the sake of obtaining linen unless I can obtain a unit of linen by foregoing *less* than a unit of china. All this may be represented very simply and clearly on our diagrams. Drawing out separately, for convenience, the curves given in Fig. 11, and making any assumptions we choose as to quantities of linen and china possessed, we may read at once (Fig. 12) the *equivalents in worth* (to the possessor) of linen and china. Thus if I have eight units of china [ϕ' (china) $= \cdot3$] and four units of linen [f' (linen) $= 1\cdot2$]; then in the limit one small unit of linen at the margin is equivalent in worth to four small units of china at the margin. If I have seven units of linen and two of china, then one small unit of china at the margin is equivalent in worth to two small units of linen at the margin.

Hitherto we have spoken of foot-tons, or generally of work, merely as a standard by which to measure a man's estimate of the various objects of his desire ; but we know, as a matter of fact, that work is often a *means of securing* these objects, and it by no means follows that

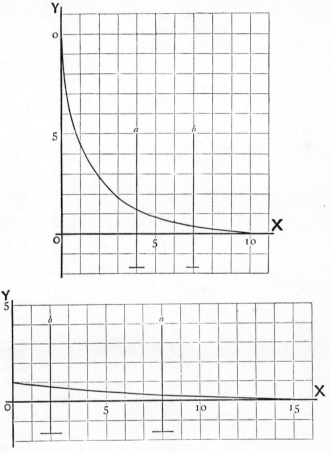

Fig. 12.

the precise amount of work a man would be willing to do rather than go without a thing is also the precise amount of work he will have to do in order to make it. Indeed there is no reason in general why a man should have to do either more or less work for the first unit of a commodity with its high utility than for the last with its comparatively low utility. The question then arises: On what principle will a man distribute his work between two objects of desire? In other words, If a man can make two different things which he wants, in what proportions will he make them?

We must begin by drawing out the curves of quantity-and-marginal-usefulness of the two commodities, and we will select as the unit on the axis of x in each case that quantity of the commodity that can be made or got by an hour's work. Suppose Robinson Crusoe* has provided himself with the absolute necessaries of life, but finds that he can vary his diet by digging for esculent roots, and can add to the comfort and beauty of his hut by gathering fresh rushes to strew on the floor two or three times a week. Adopting any arbitrary standard unit of satisfaction, let us suppose that the marginal usefulness of the roots begins at six and would be extinguished (for the week, let us say) when eight hours' work had been done. That is to say, the quantity which Robinson could dig in eight hours would absolutely satisfy him for a week, so that he would not care for more even if he could get them for nothing. In like manner let the marginal usefulness of rushes begin at four and be extinguished (for the week) by five hours' work; and let the other data be such as are depicted on the two curves in Fig. 13.† Now suppose further that Robinson can give seven hours a week to the two tasks together. How will he distribute his labour between them? If he gives four hours' work to digging for roots and three to gathering rushes, the marginal usefulness of the two articles will be measured by the vertical intercepts on a and a' respectively. Clearly there has

---

* "Political economists have always been addicted to Robinsoniads" (Marx).

† They are drawn to the formulæ—

$$y = \frac{24 - 3x}{4 + x} \text{ and } y = \frac{40 - 8x}{10 + 7x} \text{ respectively.}$$

been waste, for the latter portions of the time devoted
to rush-gathering have been devoted to producing a
thing less urgently needed than a further supply of roots.
Again, if six hours be given to digging and one to rush-
gathering, the marginal usefulness will be measured by
the vertical intercepts on b and b', and again there
has been waste, this time from excessive root digging.
But if five hours are given to digging for roots and two
to rush-gathering, the usefulness will be measured
by the vertical intercepts on c and c', and there is no
loss, for obviously any labour subtracted from either

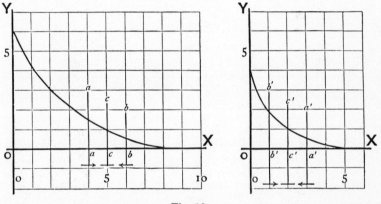

Fig. 13.

occupation and added to the other would result in the
sacrifice of a greater satisfaction than the one it secured.

It is obvious that for any given time, such as three
hours or two hours, there is a similar ideal distribution
between the two occupations which secures the maximum result in gratification of desires ; and the method
of distribution may be represented by a very simple and
beautiful graphic device, exemplified in Fig. 14.

First draw the two curves one within the other,*
then add them together sideways, so as to make a

* If the curves should cross, as in Fig. 10, the principle is entirely
unaffected.

third curve (dotted in figure), after the following fashion :
For $y = 1$ the corresponding value of x for the inner
curve is 2, and that for the outer curve 5. Adding
these two together we obtain 7 ; and for our new curve
we shall have

$$y = 1 \quad x = 7.$$

Every other point of the new curve may be found in
the same way, and we shall then have a dotted curve such
that if any line $pp_1p_2p_3$ be drawn parallel to the axis
of x, and cutting the three curves, the line p_2p_3 shall

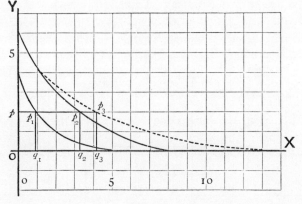

Fig. 14.

be equal to the line pp_1. We shall then have $pp_3 = pp_1$
$+ pp_2$;* and if we desire to see how Robinson will
apportion any quantity of time Oq_3 between the two
occupations we shall simply have to erect a perpendicular
at q_3, and where it cuts the dotted curve draw a parallel
to the axis of x, cutting the other curves at p_2 and p_1.
We shall then have divided the whole time of Oq_3 into

* If the curves are drawn to the formulæ $y = f(x)$ and $y = \phi(x)$ we
may express them also as $x = f^{-1}(y)$ and $x = \phi^{-1}(y)$. It is obvious
that our new curve will then be $x = f^{-1}(y) + \phi^{-1}(y)$, which in this
case will give $x = \dfrac{312 + 146y - 38y^2}{24 + 29y + 7y^2}$, to which formula the curve is drawn
between the values $y = 4$ and $y = 0$.

two parts, Oq_1 and Oq_2 ($= pp_1$ and pp_2), such that if Oq_1 is devoted to the one occupation and Oq_2 to the other the maximum satisfaction will be secured.

If we take $Oq_3 = 7$ we shall find we get $Oq_1 = 2$, $Oq_2 = 5$, as above.*

This is a principle of the utmost importance, applicable to a great variety of problems, such as the most advantageous distribution of a given quantity of any commodity between two or more different uses. It is particularly important in the pure theory of the currency. It need hardly be pointed out that these diagrams do not pretend to assist any one in practically determining how to divide his time. They are merely intended to throw light on the process by which he effects the distribution. In any concrete investigation we should have direct access to the result but not to the conditions of want and estimated satisfaction which determine it ; so that the actual distributions would be our data and the preceding conditions of desire, etc. our quæsita.

We have now reached a stage of our investigations at which it will be useful to recapitulate and expand our conclusions as to the marginal usefulness of commodities. In doing so we must bear in mind especially what has been said as to the nature of our diagrammatic curves (p. 12). The law of a curve is the law of the connection between the corresponding pairs of values of two varying quantities, one of which is a function of the other. The curve on Fig. 7, for instance, is not the "curve of the heat produced by given quantities of carbon in a furnace," nor yet the "curve of the quantities of carbon which effect given degrees of heat in a furnace," but "the curve of the connection between varying quantities of carbon burned and varying degrees

---

* Note that when the hours of work have been distributed between the two occupations they pass into concrete results in the shape of commodity. Thus, strictly speaking, we measure *hours* along the axis of *x* when dealing with the dotted curve, but *hour-results* in commodity when we come to the other curves. If $Oq_3 = 7$, then, whereas $Oq_3 = 7$ *hours*, Oq_1 and Oq_2 represent respectively 2 and 5 *units of commodity*, each unit being the result of an hour's work.

of heat produced," each of which magnitudes severally is always measured by a vertical or horizontal straight line.

In like manner, the first curve in Fig. 13 is not "the curve of the varying marginal usefulness of esculent roots to Robinson at given margins," nor "the curve of the varying quantities of esculent roots which correspond to given marginal usefulnesses," but "the curve of the connection between the quantity of roots Robinson possesses and the marginal usefuluess of roots to him."

When this fact is fully grasped it will become obvious that there are only two things which can conceivably alter the marginal usefulness of a commodity to me: either the quantity I possess must change, or the law must change which connects that quantity and the marginal usefulness of the commodity. If *both* these remain the same, obviously the marginal utility must remain the same. Or, in symbols, if $y = f(x)$* the value of y can only be altered by changing the value of x, or by changing the function signified by f. The necessity for insisting upon this axiomatic truth will become evident as we proceed. Meanwhile,

> One charge, one sovereign charge I press,
> And stamp it with reiterate stress,

viz. to bear in mind, so as to recognise it under all disguises, the fundamental and self-evident truth, that the marginal usefulness of a commodity always depends upon the quantity of the commodity possessed [$y = f(x)$], and that if the *nature of the dependence* [the form of the function f] and the quantity of the commodity possessed [the value of x] remain the same, then the marginal usefulness of the commodity [the value of y] likewise remains unchanged. Whatever changes it must

---

* Note that the symbol $f(x)$ is perfectly general, and signifies any kind of function of x. It therefore includes and may properly represent the class of functions we have hitherto represented by letters with a dash, $f'(x)$, $\phi'(x)$, etc.

do so either by changing the nature of its dependence
upon the quantity possessed or by changing that quantity itself ; nothing which cannot change either of
these can change the marginal usefulness ; and whatever changes the marginal usefulness does so by means
of changing one of these.   The length of the vertical
intercept cannot change unless *either* the course of the
curve changes *or* the position of the bearer is shifted.

These remarks, of course, apply to total utility as
well as to marginal usefulness.

Now, hitherto we have considered changes in the
quantity possessed only ; and have supposed the nature
of the connection between the quantity and the total
utility or marginal usefulness to remain constant, *i.e.*
we have shifted our bearers, but have supposed our
curves to remain fixed in their forms.   But obviously
in practical life it is quite as important to consider the
shifting of the curve as the shifting of the bearer and
the quantity-index.   To revert to our first example.
The law that connects the quantity of coal I burn with
the sum of advantages I derive from its consumption is
not the same in winter and in summer, or in the house
I now live in and the house I left ten years ago.   And
in other cases, where there is a less obvious external
cause of change, a man's tastes and desires are nevertheless perpetually varying.   The state of his health, the
state of his affections, the nature of his studies, and a
thousand other causes change the amount of enjoyment
or advantage he can derive from a given quantity of a
given commodity ; and if we wish to have an adequate
conception of the real economic conditions of life we
must not only imagine what we have called the " bearer,"
that carries the vertical or quantity-index moving freely
along the axis of *x*, but we must also imagine the form
of the curve to be perpetually flowing and changing.

The obvious impossibility of adequately representing on
diagrams the flux and change of the curves presents a great

difficulty to the demonstrator. Some attempt will here be made to convey to the reader an elementary conception of the nature of these changes.

We will take the simplest case, that of the straight line, as an illustration. Suppose (a not very probable supposition) that the quantity-and-marginal-usefulness curve of a certain commodity for a certain man at a certain time is represented by $y = 12 - 2x.$

By giving successive values to x we shall find the corre-

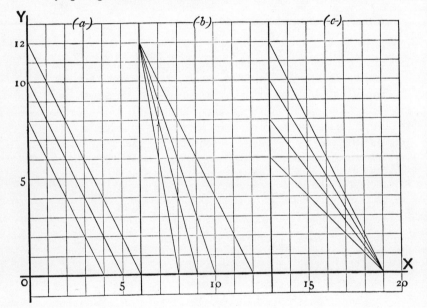

Fig. 15.

sponding values of y, and shall see that the curve is the highest of the straight lines represented on Fig. 15 (a). Now suppose that, owing to some cause or other, the man comes to need the commodity less, so that its marginal utility, while still decreasing by the same law as before, shall now begin at ten instead of twelve. The formula of the curve will then be $y = 10 - 2x$, and the curve will be the second straight line in Fig. 15 (a). By taking the formula, $y = 8 - 2x$, we may obtain yet another line, and so on indefinitely.

What we have now been doing may be represented by the formula $$y = f(z, x) = z - 2x,$$
where y is a function of two variables, namely z and x, and we proceed by giving z successive values, and then for each several value of z giving x successive values. If instead of taking the values 12, 10, 8 for z, we suppose it to pass continuously through all values, it is obvious that we should have a system of parallel straight lines, one of which would pass through any given point on the axis of x or y.

But we have supposed the modifications in the position of the line always to be of one perfectly simple character ; whereas it is easy to imagine that the man whose wants we are considering might find that for some reason he needed a smaller and smaller quantity of the commodity in question completely to satisfy his wants, whereas his initial desire remained as keen as ever. Such a case would be represented by $$y = f(z, x) = 12 - zx,$$
in which we may give z the values of 2, 3, 4, 6 successively, and then trace the lines in Fig. 15 (*b*) by making x pass through all values from 0 to $\dfrac{12}{z}$, after which the values of y would be negative.

But again we might suppose that while the quantity of the commodity needed completely to sate a man remained the same, the eagerness of his initial desire might abate. This case might be represented by

$$y = f(z, x) = z - \frac{z}{6}x,$$

where by making z successively equal to 12, 10, 8, 6, etc., we shall get a system of lines such as those in Fig. 15 (*c*).

This is very far from exhausting the different modifications our curve might undergo while still remaining a straight line. For instance we might have a series of lines, one of which should run from 12 on the axis of y to 6 on the axis of x, as before, while another ran from 8 on the axis of y to 12 on the axis of x, and so on. This would indicate that two independent causes were at work to modify the man's want for the commodity.

Passing on to a case rather less simple, we may take the first curve of Fig. 13, which was drawn to the formula

$$y = f(x) = \frac{24 - 3x}{4 + x},$$

and confining ourselves to a single modification, may regard
it as $$y = f(z, x) = \frac{24 - 3x}{z + x},$$
when, by making z successively equal 4, 6, 8, and 12, we
shall get the four curves of Fig. 16.

If we suppose that z and x are both changing at the same
time, *i.e.* that the quantity of the commodity *and* the nature
of the dependence of its marginal usefulness upon its quantity
are changing together, then the effect of the two changes
may be that each will intensify the other, or it may be that

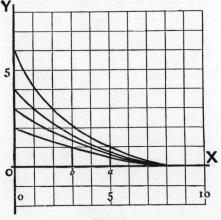

Fig. 16.

they will counteract each other. Thus in $y = f(z, x) =$
$\frac{24 - 3x}{z + x}$, if x is first 5 and then 3, while z at the same time
passes from 4 to 12, we shall have for the two values of y
$\frac{24 - 3 \times 5}{4 + 5}$ and $\frac{24 - 3 \times 3}{12 + 3}$, and in either case $y = 1$. This is
shown on the figure by the lines at a and b.

We must remember, then, that two things, and only two,
can alter the marginal usefulness of a commodity, viz. (i) a
change in its quantity and (ii) a change in the connection
between its quantity and its marginal usefulness. In the
diagrams these are represented by (i) a movement of the
"bearer" carrying the vertical to and fro on the base line,
and (ii) a change in the form or position of the curve. In

symbols they are represented (i) by a change in the value of x, and (ii) by a change in the meaning of f. Anything that changes the value of y must do so *by* changing one of these. Generally speaking the causes that affect the nature of the function (*i.e.* the shape and position of the curve), so far as they lend themselves to investigation, must be studied under the "theory of consumption ;" while an examination of the causes which affect the magnitude of x (*i.e.* the position of the "quantity-index") will include, together with other things, the "theory of production."

II

WE have seen that the most varied and heterogeneous wants and desires that exist *in one mind* or "subject" may be reduced to a common measure and compared one with another; but there is another truth which must never be lost sight of on peril of a total misconception of all the results we may arrive at in our investigations; and that is, that by no possibility can desires or wants, even for one and the same thing, which exist *in different minds*, be measured against one another or reduced to a common measure. If x, y, and z are all of them objects of desire to A, we can tell by his actions which of them he desires most, but if A, B, and C all desire x no possible process can determine which of them desires it most. For any method of investigation is open to the fatal objection that it must use as a standard of measurement something that may not mean the same in the different minds to be compared. Lady Jane Grey studies Plato while her companions ride in Bradgate Park, whence we learn that an hour's study was more than an equivalent to the ride to Lady Jane and less than its equivalent to the others. But who is to tell us whether Greek gave *her* more pleasure than hunting gave *them?* Lady Jane fancied it did, but she may have been mistaken. My account-book, intelligently studied, may tell you a good deal as to the equivalence of various pleasures and comforts to me, but it can establish no kind of equation between the amount of pleasure which I derive from a certain article and the

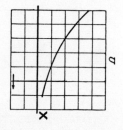

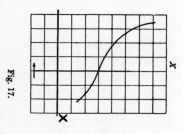

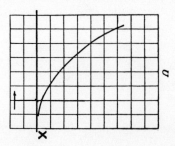

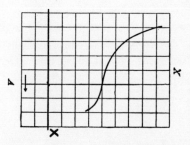

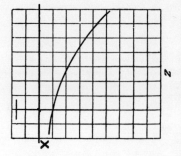

Fig. 17.

To face page 69.

amount of pleasure you would derive from it. *B* wears his black coats out to the bitter end and goes shabby three months in every year in order to get a few pounds worth of books per annum. *A* would never think of doing so—but whether because he values books less or a genteel appearance more than *B* does not appear. Nay, it is even possible he values books more, but that his sensitiveness in the matter of clothing exceeds *B*'s in a still higher degree. *C* may be willing to wait three hours at the door of a theatre to get a place, whereas *D* will not wait more than ten minutes; but this does not show that *C* wants to witness the representation more than *D* does; it may be that *D* has less physical endurance than *C*, and would suffer severely from the exhaustion of long waiting; or it may be that *C* has nothing particular to do with his time and so does not value it as much as *D* does his.

Look at it how we will, then, it is impossible to establish any scientific comparison between the wants and desires of two or more separate individuals. Yet it is obvious that almost the whole field of economic investigation is concerned with collective wants and desires; and we shall constantly have to speak of the relative intensity of the demand for different articles or commodities not on the part of this or that individual, but on the part of society in general. In like manner we shall speak of the marginal usefulness and utility of such and such an article, not for the individual but for the community at large. What right have we to use such language, and what must we take it to mean?

To answer this question satisfactorily we must make the relative intensity of the desires and wants of the individual our starting-point. Let us suppose that *A* possesses stocks of U, V, W, X, Y, Z, the marginal utility to him of the customary unit (pound, yard, piece, bushel, hundredweight, or whatever it may be) of each of these articles being such that, calling a unit of U, *u*, a unit of V, *v*, etc., we shall have $3u$ or $10v$ or $4w$ or

$\dfrac{x}{4}$ or $\dfrac{3y}{2}$, applied at the margin, just equivalent to z (*i.e.*
one unit of Z) at the margin. Portions of arbitrary
curves illustrating the supposed cases of U, X, and Z
are given in Fig. 17 (A). The curves represent the marginal usefulness per unit of U as being one-third as great
as that of Z. That is to say, if u is but a very small
fraction of A's whole stock of U, then, in the limit, $3u = z$.
In like manner $\dfrac{x}{4} = z$, in the limit. Now let us .take
another man, B. We may find that he does not possess
(and possibly is not aware of definitely desiring) any V,
W, or Y at all; but we will suppose that he possesses
stocks of U, X, and Z. In this case (neglecting the
practically very important element of friction) we shall
find that the units of U, X, and Z stand in exactly the
same *relative* positions for him as they do for A ; that is
to say, we shall find that for B, as for A, $3u$ or $\dfrac{x}{4}$ is exactly equivalent to z. For were it otherwise the conditions for a mutually advantageous exchange would
obviously be present.

Suppose, for instance, we have

$$\dfrac{x}{3} \text{ equivalent to } 2u \qquad \text{for } B,$$

as represented in Fig 17 (B), while

$$\dfrac{x}{4} \text{ is equivalent to } 3u \qquad \text{for } A,$$

as before. Then, reducing to more convenient forms,*
we shall have

$$6u \text{ equivalent to } x \qquad \text{for } B,$$
$$12u \text{ equivalent to } x \qquad \text{for } A.$$

Observe that though we may suppose there will frequently
be some general similarity of form between the curves that

---

* This process is legitimate if x and u are "small" units of X and
U, so that the marginal usefulness of U remains sensibly constant
throughout the consumption of $3u$, etc.

connect the quantity of U with its marginal usefulness in the cases of A and B respectively, yet we have no right whatever to assume any close resemblance between these curves.

Now since six units of U are equivalent to a unit of X for B, he will evidently be glad to receive anything *more than six* units of U in exchange for a unit of X; whereas A will be glad to give *anything less than twelve* units of U for a unit of X. The precise terms on which we may expect the exchange to take place will not be investigated here, but it is obvious that there is a wide margin for an arrangement by which A can give U in exchange for X from B, to the mutual advantage of the two parties. The result of such an exchange will be to change the quantities and make the quantity indices move in the directions indicated by the arrow heads; A's stock of U decreasing and his stock of X increasing, while B's stock of U increases and his stock of X decreases. But this very process tends to bring the ratio $\dfrac{\text{marginal usefulness of U}}{\text{marginal usefulness of X}}$ or $\dfrac{\text{marginal utility of } u}{\text{marginal utility of } x}$ nearer to unity (*i.e.* increase it) for A, for whom it is now $\frac{1}{12}$, and to remove it farther from unity (*i.e.* decrease it) for B, to whom it is now $\frac{1}{6}$. This is obvious from a glance at the figures or a moment's reflection on what they represent. Using $\dfrac{u}{x}$ as a symbol of $\dfrac{\text{marginal utility of } u}{\text{marginal utility of } x}$ we may, therefore, say that the ratio $\dfrac{u}{x}$ will increase for A, to whom it is now lowest, and decrease for B, to whom it is now highest. If this movement continues long enough,* there must come a point at which $\dfrac{u}{x}$ will be the same for A and B. Now until this point is reached the causes which produce

* Compare below, p. 73 and the note.

the motion towards it continue to be operative, for it is always possible to imagine a ratio of exchange $\frac{u}{x}$ which shall be greater than A's $\frac{u}{x}$ and less than B's $\frac{u}{x}$, and shall therefore be advantageous to both. But when A's $\frac{u}{x}$ and B's $\frac{u}{x}$ have met there will be equilibrium. Hence if the *relative* worth, at the margin, of units of any two commodities U and X should not be identical for two persons A and B, the conditions of a profitable exchange between them exist, and continue to exist, until the resultant changes have brought about a state of equilibrium, in which the relative worths, at the margin, of units of the two commodities are identical for the two individuals.

This proposition is of such crucial and fundamental importance that we will repeat the demonstration with a more sparing use of symbols, and without reference to the figures.

B, who is glad to get anything more than $6u$ for x, and A, who is glad to give anything short of $12u$ for x, exchange U and X to their mutual advantage, B getting U and giving X, while A gets X and gives U.

But by this very act of exchange B's stock of X is decreased and his stock of U increased, and thereby the marginal usefulness of X is raised and that of U lowered, so that B will now find $6u$ less than the equivalent of x; or in other words, the interval between the worth of a unit of X and that of a unit of U is increasing, and at the same time A's stock of X is increasing and his stock of U diminishing, whereby the marginal usefulness of U increases and that of X diminishes, so that now less than twelve units of U are needed to make an equivalent to one unit of X; or in other words, the interval between the worths at the margin of a unit of U and a unit of X is diminishing. To begin with, then,

u and x differ less in worth, at the margin, to B than they do to A, but the difference in worth to B is constantly increasing and that to A constantly diminishing as the exchange goes on. There must, therefore, come a point at which the expanding smaller difference and the contracting greater difference will coincide.* The conditions for a profitable exchange will then cease to exist ; but at the same moment the marginal worths of u and x will come to stand in precisely the same ratio for A and for B. Wherever, then, articles possessed in common by A and B differ in the ratio of their unitary marginal utilities as estimated by A and B, the conditions of a profitable exchange exist, and this exchange itself tends to remove the difference which gives rise to it. We may take it, then, that in a state of equilibrium the ratios of the unitary marginal utilities of any articles, X, Y, Z, etc., possessed in common by A, B, C, etc., taken two by two, viz. $x : y$, $x : z$, $y : z$, etc., *are severally identical for all the possessors.* Any departure from this state of equilibrium tends to correct itself by giving rise to exchanges that restore the equilibrium on the same or another basis.

To give precision and firmness to this conception, we may work it out a little farther. Let us call such a table as the one given on pp. 69, 70 a "scale of the relative unitary marginal utilities to A of the commodities he possesses," or briefly, "A's relative scale." How shall we bring the relative scales of B, C, etc. into the form most convenient for comparison with A's ? In A's relative scale the unitary marginal utilities of all the articles, that is to say, u, v, w, x, y, z, were expressed in terms of the unitary marginal utility of Z, that is to say, z. And in like manner B's relative scale expressed u and x in terms of z. But now suppose C possesses S, T, V, X, and Y, but no U, W, or Z. It is obvious that, in so far as he possesses the same commodities as A and B, his relative

---

* Unless, indeed, the whole stock of A's X or of B's U is exhausted before equilibrium is reached. See p. 82.

scale, when there is equilibrium, must coincide with theirs. But when we attempt to draw out that scale by direct reference to *B*'s wants, we find ourselves unable to express the unitary marginal utilities of his commodities in terms of the unitary marginal utility of Z, for since he has no Z (and perhaps does not want any) we cannot ask him to estimate its marginal usefulness to him.* But it is obvious that *A*'s scale fixes the relative marginal utilities of the units *v*, *x*, and *y* in terms of each other as well as in terms of *z*, and unless they are the same to *C* that they are to *A* the conditions of an advantageous exchange between *A* and *C* will arise and will continue till *v*, *x*, *y* coincide on the two relative scales. In like manner *B*'s scale expresses the marginal utilities of the units *s* and *t* in terms of each other, and *C*'s scale must, when there is equilibrium, coincide with *B*'s in respect of these two units. Now, even though *C* not only possesses no Z, but does not even desire any, there is nothing to prevent him, for convenience of transactions with *A* and *B*, from estimating *s*, *t*, *v*, *x*, and *y* not in terms of each other, but in terms of *z*, placing it hypothetically in his own scale in the same place relatively to the other units which it occupies for *A* and *B*. Thus he may express his desire for the commodities he has or wants to have, in terms of a desire to which he is himself a stranger, but the relative strength of which in other men's minds he has been able to ascertain.

Lastly, if *C* knows that he can at any time get S and T from *B*, and V, X and Y from *A*, in exchange for Z, on definite terms of exchange, then, although he may not want Z for himself, and may have no possible use for it, yet he will be glad to get it, though only as representing the things he does want, and for which he

---

* We shall see presently (p. 82) that the estimate must positively be made in terms of a commodity possessed, and that even if *B* wants Z, and knows exactly how much he wants a first unit of it, that want will not serve as the standard unit of desire unless he actually possesses some quantity of Z.

will immediately exchange it, unless indeed he finds it more convenient to keep a stock of Z on hand ready to exchange for S, T, etc. as he wants them for actual consumption than to keep those commodities themselves in any large quantities.

All this is exactly what really takes place. Gold (in England) is the Z adopted for purposes of reference (and also, though less exclusively, as a vehicle of exchange). Gold is valuable for many purposes in the arts and sciences, and, therefore, there are always a number of persons who want gold to use, and will give other things in exchange for it. Most of us possess, and use in a very direct manner, a small quantity of gold which we could not dispense with without great immediate suffering and the risk of serious ultimate detriment to our health, viz., the gold stoppings of some of our teeth. There is a constant demand for gold for this use. Lettering and ornamenting the backs of books is another use of gold in which vast numbers of persons have an immediate interest as consumers. Plate and ornaments are a more obvious if not more important means of employing gold for the direct gratification of human desires or supply of human wants. In short, there are a great number of well-known and easily accessible persons who, for one purpose or another of direct use or enjoyment, desire gold, and since these persons desire many other things also, their wants furnish a scale on which the unitary marginal utilities of a great variety of articles are registered in terms of the unitary marginal utility of gold, and if the relative scales of any two of these gold-and-other-commodities-desiring individuals differ, then exchanges will be made until they coincide. Other persons who have no direct desire or use for gold desire a number of the other commodities which find a place in the scale of the gold-desiring persons, and can, therefore, compare the relative positions they occupy in their own scale of desires with that which is assigned them in the scale of the gold-desiring people, and if these relative positions vary exchanges may advantageously be made until they coincide.   Thus the non-gold-desiring people may find it convenient to express their desires in terms of the gold-desire to which they are themselves strangers, and seeing that the gold-desiring people are accessible and numerous, even those who have no real personal gold-desire will always value gold, because they can always get what they want in exchange for it from the gold-desiring people.   Indeed, as soon as this fact is generally known and realised, people will generally find it convenient to keep a certain portion of their possessions not in the form of anything they really want, but in the form of gold.

We may, therefore, measure all concrete utilities in terms of gold, and so compare them one with another. Only we must remember that by this means we reach a purely objective and material scale of equivalence, and that the fact that I can get a sovereign for either of two articles does not prove, or in any way tend to prove, that the two articles really confer equivalent benefits, *unless it is the same man who is willing to give a sovereign for either.*

A's and *B*'s desires for U and W, when measured in their respective desires for Z, are indeed equivalent; but the *measure itself* may mean to the two men things severed by a hell-wide chasm; for *A*'s desire for U, W, and Z alike may be satisfied almost to the point of satiety, so that an extra unit of Z would hardly confer any perceptible gratification upon him; whereas *B* may be in extreme need alike of U, W, and Z, so that an extra unit of Z would minister to an almost unendurable craving.

Or again, *A* may possess certain commodities, V, X, Y, which *B* does not possess, and is not conscious of wanting at all (say billiard tables, pictures by old masters, and fancy ball costumes), and in like manner *B* may possess W and T (say corduroy breeches and

tripe), which A neither possesses nor desires. Now in
B's scale of marginal utilities we may find that $t = \dfrac{z}{80}$
(taking $t =$ one cut of tripe, and $z =$ the gold in a
sovereign),* whereas in B's scale one $v = 50z$.   Then
taking one z as a purely objective standard, and neglecting the difference of its meaning to the two men, and
regarding A and B as forming a "community," we
might say that in that community $z = 80t$ and $v = 50z$,
or $v = 4000t$, i.e. one v is worth 4000 times as much as
one t. By this we should mean that the man in the
community who wants Z will give 4000 times as much
for a unit of it as you can get out of the man who
wants T in exchange for a unit of that. But this does
not even tend to show that a unit of V will give the
man who wants it 4000 times the pleasure which the
other man would derive from a unit of T. Nay, it is
quite possible that the latter satisfaction might be positively the greater of the two.

Note, then, that the function of gold, or money, as a
standard, is to reduce all kinds of services and commodities
to an objective scale of equivalence ; and this constitutes its
value in commercial affairs, and at the same time explains
the instinctive dislike of money dealings with friends which
many men experience. Money is the symbol of the exact
balancing and setting off one against the other of services
rendered or goods exchanged ; and this balancing can only
be affected by absolutely renouncing all attempts to arrive at
a *real* equivalence of effort or sacrifice, and adopting in its
place an external and mechanical equivalence which has no
tendency to conform to the real equivalence. It is the
systematising of the individualistic point of view which says,
" One unit of Z may be a very different thing for A or B to
give, but it is exactly the same thing for me to *get*, wherever

---

* These cannot be regarded as "small" units in the technical
sense, in this case. We are speaking in this example strictly of the
values of units at the margin, and they will not coincide even roughly
with the ideal "usefulness" of the commodity at the margin.

it comes from ; and, therefore, I regard it as the same thing all the world over, and measure all that I get or give in terms of it." Where the relations to be regulated are themselves prevailingly external and objective, this plan works excellently. But amongst friends, and wherever friendship or any high degree of conscious and active goodwill enters into the relations to be regulated, two things are felt. In the first place we do not wish to keep an evenly balanced account, and to set services, etc., against each other, but we wish to act on the principle of the mutual gratuitousness of services; and in the second place, so far as any idea of a rough equivalence enters our minds at all, we are not satisfied with anything but a real equivalence, an equivalence, that is, of sacrifice or effort ; and this may depart indefinitely from the objective equivalence in gold. This also explains the dislike of money and money dealings which characterises such saints as St. Francis of Assisi. Money is the incarnate negation of their principle of mutual gratuitousness of service.

Under what circumstances the objective scale might be supposed roughly, and taken over a wide area, to coincide with the real scale, we shall ask presently. If such circumstances were realised, and in as far as they actually are realised, it is obvious that the objective scale has a social and moral, as well as a commercial, value. (Compare p. 86.)

In future we may speak of a man's desire or want of "gold" without implying that he has any literal gold-desire at all, but using the "unitary marginal utility of gold" as the standard unit of desire, and expressing the (objective) intensity of any man's want of anything in terms of that unit. It is abundantly obvious from what has gone before in what way we shall reduce to this unit the wants of a man who has no real desire for gold at all. When we use gold in this extended and representative sense we shall indicate the fact by putting it in quotation marks : "gold." Thus any one who possesses anything at all must to that extent possess "gold," though he may be entirely without gold.

The result we have now reached is of the utmost importance. We have shown that in any catallactic community,* when in the state of equilibrium, the marginal utilities of units of all the commodities that enter into the circle of exchange will arrange themselves on a certain relative scale or table in which any one of them can be expressed in terms of any other, and that that scale will be general; that is to say, it will accurately translate or express, *for each individual in the community*, the worth at the margin of a unit of any of the commodities he possesses, in terms of any other.

The scope and significance of this result will become more and more apparent as we proceed; but we can already see that the desiredness at the margin of a unit of any commodity, expressed in terms of the desiredness at the margin of a unit of any other commodity, is the same thing as the *value-in-exchange* (or exchange-value) of the first commodity expressed in terms of the second.

We have therefore established a precise relation between value-in-use and value-in-exchange; for we have discovered that the value-in-exchange of an article conforms to the place it occupies on the (necessarily coincident) relative scales of all the persons in the community who possess it. Now to every man the marginal utility of an article, that is to say of a unit of any commodity, is determined by the average between the marginal usefulness of the commodity at the beginning and its marginal usefulness at the end of the acquisition of that unit; and this marginal usefulness itself is the first derived function, or the differential coefficient, of the total utility of the stock of the commodity, which the man possesses. Or briefly, *the value-in-exchange of a commodity is the differential coefficient of the total utility, to each member of the community, of the stock of the commodity he possesses.*

"The things which have the greatest value-in-use

---

* I mean by a catallactic community one in which the individuals freely exchange commodities one with another, each with a view to making the enjoyment he derives from his possessions a maximum.

have frequently little or no value-in-exchange; and, on the contrary, those which have the greatest value-in-exchange have frequently little or no value-in-use. Nothing is more useful than water; but it will purchase scarce anything; scarce anything can be had in exchange for it" (Adam Smith). Now that we know exchange-value to be measured by marginal usefulness, we can well understand this fact. For as the total value in use of a thing approaches its maximum its exchange-value tends to disappear. Were water less abundant its value-in-use would be reduced, but its exchange-value would be so much increased that there would be "scarce anything that could not be had in exchange for it." As it is the total effect of water is so near its maximum that its effectiveness at the margin is comparatively small.

Before proceeding farther we will look somewhat more closely into this matter of the identity of the exchange-value of a unit of any commodity and its desiredness at the margin of the stocks of the persons who possess it.

In practical life, if I say that the exchange-value of a horse is £31, I am either speaking from the point of view of a buyer, and mean that a horse of a certain quality could be got in exchange for 8 oz. of gold;* or I am speaking from the point of view of a seller, and mean that a man could get 8 oz. of gold for the horse; but I cannot mean both, for notoriously (if all the conditions remain the same) the buying and selling prices are never identical. What then do I mean when, speaking as an economist, I suppose, without further specification, that the exchange-value of a horse in ounces of gold is 8 ? I mean that the offer of anything *more* than the 8 oz. of gold for a horse of the quality specified will *tend to induce* some possessor of such a horse to part with him, and the offer of such a horse for anything *less* than 8 oz. of gold will *tend to induce* some possessor of gold to take the horse in exchange for some of it; and if I reduce the friction

* About 7·97 oz. of gold is contained in £31.

of exchange (both physical and mental) towards the vanishing point, I may say that every man who is willing to give *any* more than 8 oz. of gold for a horse can get him, and every man who is willing to take *any* less than 8 oz. of gold for a horse can sell him.

The exchange-value of a horse, then, in ounces of gold, represents a quantity of gold such that a man can get anything short of it for a horse, and can get a horse for anything above it. And obviously, if the conditions remain the same, every exchange will tend to destroy the conditions under which exchanges will take place, for after each exchange the number of people who desire to exchange on terms which will "induce business" tends to be reduced by two.

Thus if the exchange value of a horse is 8 oz. of gold, that means that the ratio " 1 horse to 8 oz. gold " is a point *on either side of which* exchanges will take place, each exchange, however, tending to produce an equilibrium on the attainment of which exchange will cease.

Now we have shown in detail that the relative scale of marginal utilities is a table of precisely such ratios, between units of all commodities that enter into the circle of exchange. Any departure in the relative scale of any individual from these ratios will at once induce exchanges that will tend to restore equilibrium. We find, then, that the relative scale is, in point of fact, *a table of exchange values*, and that the exchange value of an article is simply its marginal utility measured in the marginal utility of the commodity selected as the standard of value. And, after all, this is no more than the simplest dictate of common sense and experience ; for we have seen that the conditions of exchange are that some one should be willing, as a matter of business, to give more (or take less) than 8 oz. of gold for a horse; but what could induce that willingness except the fact that the marginal utility of a horse is greater, to the man in question, than the marginal utility of 8 oz. gold ? And what should

induce any other man to do business with him except
the fact that to that other man the marginal utility of a
horse is *not* greater than that of 8 oz. of gold ? In other
words, the conditions of exchange only exist when there
is a discrepancy in the relative scales of two individuals
who belong to the same community; and, as we have seen,
the exchange itself tends to remove this discrepancy.

Thus, *the function of exchange is to bring the relative
scales of all the individuals of a catallactic community into
correspondence*, and the equilibrium-ratio of exchange
between any two commodities is the ratio which exists
between their unitary marginal utilities when this correspondence has been established. Thus if the machinery
of exchange were absolutely perfect, then, *given the
initial possessions of each individual in the community*, there
would be such a redistribution of them that no two men
who could derive mutual satisfaction from exchanges
would fail to find each other out ; and so in a certain
sense the satisfactions of the community would be
maximised by the flow of all commodities from the
place in which they were relatively less to the place in
which they were relatively more valued. But the conformity of the net result to any principle of justice or
of public good *would depend entirely on initial conditions*
prior to all exchange.

It must never be forgotten that the coincident relative
scales of the individuals who make up a community
severally contain the things actually possessed (or commanded) only, not all the things *wanted* by the respective
individuals. If a man's *initial* want of X relatively to
his (marginal) want of "gold" is not so great as the
marginal want of X relatively to the (marginal) want of
gold experienced by the possessors of X, then he will not
come into the possession of X at all, and all that we
shall learn from the fact of his having no X, together
with an inspection of the position of X in the relative
scale of marginal utilities, is that he desires X with less
relative intensity than its possessors do. But this does

not by any means prove that his actual want of X is less pressing than theirs.   It may very well be that he wants X far more than they do, but seeing that he has very little of anything at all, his want of "gold" exceeds theirs in a still higher degree.   And, again, if one man wants X but does not want Y, and another wants Y but does not want X, and if the man who wants X wants it more, relatively to "gold," than the man who wants Y, it does not in the least follow that the one wants X absolutely more than the other wants Y, for we have no means of comparing the want of "gold" in the two cases, so that we measure the want of X and the want of Y in two units that have not been brought into any relation with each other.   All this is only to say that because I cannot "afford to buy" a thing it does not follow that I have less need of it or less desire to have it than another man who can and does afford it.

Obvious as this is, it is constantly overlooked in amateur attempts "to apply the principles of political economy to the practical problems of life."   We are told, for instance, that where there is no "demand" for a thing it shows that no one really wants it.   But before we can assent to this proposition we must know what is meant by "demand."

Now if I want a thing that I have not got, there are many ways of "demanding" it.   I may beg for it.   I may try to make people uncomfortable by forcing the extremity of my want upon them.   I may try to terrify them into giving me what I want.   I may attempt to seize it.   I may offer something for it which stands lower than it on the relative scale of marginal utilities in my community.   I may offer to work for it.   All these forms of "demand," and many more, the economists have with fine, if unconscious, irony classed together under one negative description.   Not one of them constitutes an "effective" demand.   An "effective" demand (generally described, with the omission of the adjective, as "demand" simply) is that demand, and

that demand only, which expresses itself in the offer in
exchange for the thing demanded of something else that
stands at least as high as it does on the relative scale of
marginal utilities.   No demand which expresses itself in
any language other than such an offer is recognised as a
demand at all—it is not "effective."   Now this phraseology is convenient enough in economic treatises, but
unhappily the lay disciples of the economists have a
tendency to adopt their conclusions and then discard
their definitions.   Thus they learn that it is waste of
effort to produce a commodity or render a service which
is less wanted than some other commodity or service
that would demand no greater expenditure (whether of
money, time, toil, or what not) ; they learn that what
men want most they will give most for ; and the conclusion which seems obvious is announced in such terms
as these : "Political economy shows that it is a mistake
and a waste to produce or provide anything for people
which they are not willing to pay for at a fair remuner-
ative rate ;" or, "It is false political economy to sub-
sidise anything, for if people won't pay for a thing it
shows they don't want it."   Of course political economy
does not really teach any such thing, for if it did it
would teach that a poor man never "wants" food as
much as a rich one, that a poor man never "wants" a
holiday as much as a rich one ; in a word, that a man who
has not much of anything at all has nearly as much of
everything as he wants—which is shown by his being
willing to give so very little for some more.

The fallacy, of course, lies in the use made of the
assertion that "what men want most they will give most
for."   This is true only if we are always speaking of the
same men, or if we have found a measure which can
determine which of two different men is really giving
"most."   Neither of these conditions is fulfilled in the
case we are dealing with.   "When two men give the
same thing, it is not the same thing they give," and if
A spends £100 on a continental tour and *B* half a crown

on a day at the sea-side no one can say, or without
further examination can even guess, which of them has
given "most" for his holiday.

Again, some confusion may be introduced into our
thoughts by the fact that desires not immediately backed by
any "effective" demand for gratification sometimes succeed in
getting themselves indirectly registered by means of secondary
desires which they beget in the minds of well-disposed
persons who are in a position to give "effect" to them.
Thus we may suppose that Sarah Bernhardt is charging three
hundred guineas as her fee for reciting at an evening party,
and that the three hundred guineas would provide a weeks'
holiday in the country for six hundred London children. A
benevolent and fashionable gentleman is in doubt which of
these two methods of spending the sum in question he shall
adopt, and after much debate internal makes his selection.
What do we learn from his decision ? We learn whether *his*
desire to give his friends the treat of hearing the recitation or
to give the children the benefit of country air is the greater.
It tells us nothing whatever of the relative intensity of the
desire of the guests to hear the recitation and of the children
to breathe the purer air. The primary desires concerned have
not registered their relative intensities at all, it is only the
secondary desires which they beget in the benevolent host
that register themselves ; and if the result proclaims the fact
that the marginal utility of a recitation from the tragic
actress is just six hundred times as great as the marginal
utility of a week in the country to a sick child, this does not
mean that the pleasure or advantage conferred on the company by the recitation is (or is expected to be) six hundred
times as great as that conferred upon each child by the holiday ; nor does it mean that the company would have estimated their pleasure in their own "gold" at the same sum
as that at which the six hundred children would have estimated their pleasure in their "gold," but that the host's
desire to give the pleasure to the company is as great as
his desire to give the pleasure to the six hundred children.
And since we have supposed the host's desires to be the
only "effective" ones, they alone are commercially significant.
No kind of equation—not even an objective one—is estab-

lished between the primary desires in question, viz. those of the guests and of the children respectively.*

The exchange value, then, of any commodity or service indicates its position on *its possessors'* relative scale of unitary marginal utilities; and if expressed in " gold " it indicates the ratio between the unitary marginal desiredness of the commodity and that of "gold" upon all the (necessarily coincident) relative scales of *all the members of the community who possess it.*

I have repeatedly insisted on the fact that we have no common measure by which we can compare the necessities, wants, or desires of one man with those of another. We cannot even say that " a shilling is worth more to a poor man than to a rich one," if we mean to enunciate a rule that can be safely applied to individual cases. The most we can say is, that a shilling is worth more to a man *when he is poor* than (*cæteris paribus*) to *the same man* when he is rich.

But if we take into account the principle of averages, by which any purely personal variations may be assumed to neutralise each other over any considerable area, then we may assert that shillings either are or ought to be worth more to poor men than to rich. I say " either are or ought to be ;" for it is obvious that the rich man already has his desires gratified to a greater extent than the poor man, and if in spite of that they still remain as clamorous for one shilling's worth more of satisfaction, it must be because his tastes are so much more developed and his sensitiveness to gratification has become so much finer that his organism even when its most imperative claims are satisfied still remains more sensitive to satisfactions of various kinds than the other's. But if the poor man owes his comparative freedom

---

* It is interesting to note that there are considerable manufactures of things the direct desire for which seldom or never asserts itself at all. There are immense masses of tracts and Bibles produced, for instance, which are paid for by persons who do not desire to use them but to give them away to other persons whose desire for them is not in any way an effective factor in the proceeding. And there are numbers of expensive things made expressly to be bought for " presents," and which no sane person is ever expected to buy for himself.

from desires to a low development and blunted powers, then
the very fact that though he has so few shillings yet one in
addition would be worth no more to him than to his richer
neighbour is itself the indication of social pressure and
inequality. On the assumption, then, that the humanity of
all classes of society ought ideally to receive equal development, we may say that shillings either are or ought to be
worth more to poor men than to rich. Thus, if A manufactures articles which fetch 1s. each in the open market and
are used principally by rich men, and if B produces articles
which fetch the same price but are principally consumed by
poor men, then the commercial equivalence of the two wares
does not indicate a social equivalence, i.e. it does not indicate
that the two articles confer an equal benefit or pleasure on
the community. On the contrary, if the full humanity of
B's customers has not been stunted, then his wares are of
higher social significance than A's.

It is obvious, too, that if C's wares are such as rich and
poor consume alike, the different lots which he sells to his
different customers, though each commercially equivalent to
the others, perform different services to the opulent and the
needy respectively.

Now, anything which tends to the more equal distribution
of wealth tends to remove these discrepancies. Obviously if
all were equally rich the neutralising, over a wide area, of
individual variations would take full effect ; and if a thousand
men were willing to give a shilling for A's article and five
hundred to give a shilling for B's, it would be a fair assumption that though fewer men wanted B's wares than A's, yet
those who did want them wanted them (at the margin) as
much ; nor would there be any reason to suppose that different lots of the same ware ministered, as a rule, to widely
different intensities of marginal desire ; the irreducible variations of personal constitution and habit being the only
source of inequality left.

It is true that the desire for A's and B's wares might not
be equally legitimate, from a moral point of view. I may
" want" a shameful and hurtful thing as much as I " want "
a beautiful and useful one. The State usually steps in to
say that certain wants must not be provided for at all—in
England the " want " of gaming tables, for instance—and a

man's own conscience may preclude him from supplying many other wants. But on the supposition we are now making equal intensity of commercial demand would at least represent (what no one can be sure that it represents now) equal intensity of desire on the part of the persons respectively supplied. If wealth were more equally distributed, therefore, it would be nearer the truth than it now is to say that when we supply what will sell best we are supplying what is wanted most.

These considerations are the more important because, in general, this index of price is almost the only one we can have to guide us as to what really is most wanted. When we enter into any extensive relations with men of whom we have little personal knowledge it is impossible that we should form a satisfactory opinion as to the real " equivalence" of services between ourselves and them, and it would be an immense social and moral amelioration of our civilised life if we could have some assurance that a moderate conformity existed, over every considerable area, between the price a thing would fetch and the intensity of the marginal want of it. This would be an " economic harmony " of inestimable importance. Within the narrower area of close and intimate personal relations attempts would still be made, as now, to get behind the mere " averaging " process and consider the personal wants and capacities of the individuals, the ideal being for each to " contribute according to his powers and receive according to his needs." Thus the different principles of conducting the affairs of business and of home would remain in force, but instead of their being, as they are now, in many respects opposed to each other the principles of business would be a first approximation—the closest admitted by the nature of the case—to the principles on which we deal with family and friends.

Now certain social reformers have imagined an economic Utopia in which an equal distribution of wealth, such as we have been contemplating, would be brought about as follows:— Certain industrial, social and political forces are supposed to be at work which will ultimately throw the opportunities of acquiring manual and mental skill completely open ; and skill will then cease to be a monopoly. Seeing, then, that there will only be a small number of persons incapable of doing anything but heaving, it will follow that the greater part of the heaving work of the world will be done by persons capable of doing skilled work. And hence again it will follow that every skilled task may be estimated in the foot-tons, which would be regarded by a heaver as its equivalent in irksomeness. And if we ask "What heaver?" the answer will be "The man at present engaged in heaving who estimates the relative irksomeness of the skilled task most lightly, and would therefore be most ready to take it up." Then the reward, or wages, for doing the task in question will be the same as for doing its equivalent (so defined) in foot-tons. If more were offered some of the present heavers would apply. If less were offered some of those now engaged in the skilled work would do heaving instead. To me personally heaving may be impossible or highly distasteful, but as long as some of my colleagues in my task are capable of heaving and some of the heavers capable of doing my task, a scale of equivalence will be established at the margin between them, and this will fix the scale of remuneration. Thus earnings will tend to equality with efforts, estimated in foot-tons.

From this it would follow that inequalities of earnings could not well be greater than the natural inequalities of mere brute strength; for since foot-tons of labour-power are the ultimate measure of all remunerated efforts, he who has most foot-tons of labour-power at his disposal is potentially the largest earner.

Again, the reformers who look forward to this state of things hold that forces are already at work which will ultimately dry up all sources of income except earnings, so that we shall not only have earnings proportional to efforts, estimated in foot-tons, but also incomes proportional to earnings. Thus inequalities in the distribution of wealth will be restrained within the limits of inequalities of original endowment in strength.

The speculative weakness of this Utopia obviously lies in its taking no sufficient account of differences of personal ability. Throwing open opportunities might level the rank and fill up all trades, including skilled craftsmen, artists, and heavers; but it would hardly tend to diminish the distance, for example, between the mere "man who can paint" and the great artist.

Nevertheless it is interesting to inquire how things would go in such a Utopia. In the first place we are obviously as far as ever from having established any common measure between man and man or any abstract reign of justice ; for a foot-ton is not the same thing to A and to B, neither is there any justice in a strong man having more comforts than a weak one.

Nevertheless there would be greater equality. For the number of individual families whose "means" in foot-tons of labour-power lie near about the average means, is much greater than the number of families whose present means in "gold" lie near the average means. As this statement deals with a subject on which there is a good deal of loose and inaccurate thought, it may be well to expand the conception.

If $\dfrac{a+b+c+d+e}{5}$ remains the same, then the arithmetical average of the five quantities remains the same. Suppose that average is 200. Then we may have $a=b=c=d=e=200$, or we may have $a=996$, $b=c=d=e=1$, or $a=394$, $b=202$, $c=198$, $d=200$, $e=6$. In all these cases the average is 200, but in the second case not one of the several quantities lies anywhere near the average. So again, if we pass from the case $a=b=c=d=e=200$ to the case $a=997$, $b=c=d=e=1$, we shall actually have raised the average, but we shall have removed each quantity, severally, immensely farther away from that average.

Now if we reflect that the average income of a family of five in the United Kingdom is estimated at £175 per annum, it is obvious that an enormous number of families have incomes a long way below the average. It is held to be self-evident that a smaller number of families fall conspicuously short of the average means in labour-power.

Further, the extremes evidently lie within less distance of the average in the case of labour-power than in the case of "gold." There are, it is true, some families of extraordinary athletic power, races of cricketers, oarsmen, runners, and so forth, but if we imagine such a family, while still remaining an industrial unit, to contain six or seven members each able to do the work of a whole average family, we shall probably have already exceeded the limit of legitimate speculation, and this would give six or seven times the average as the upper limit. Whereas the average "gold" income (as given

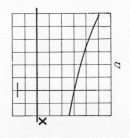
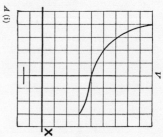

A (i)

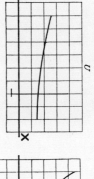
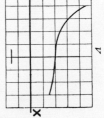

A (ii)

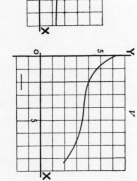

B (i)

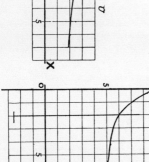

B (ii)

Fig. 18.

To face page 91.

above) being £175, we have only to think of the incomes of our millionaires to see how much further above the average the upper limit of "gold" incomes rises than it could possibly do in the case of labour-power.

The lower limit being zero in both cases does not lend itself to this comparison.

It may be urged, further, that there is no such broad distinction between the goods required by the strong (? skates, bicycles, etc.) and those required by the "weak" (? respirators, reading-chairs, etc.) as there is between those demanded by the "rich" and those demanded by the "poor." So that the analogue of the cases mentioned on p. 87 would hardly occur ; especially when we take into account the balancing effect of the association of strong and weak in the same family.

The whole of this inquiry may be epitomised and elucidated by a diagramatic illustration.

The unitary marginal utilities of U and V stand in the ratio of 3 : 4 on the relative scale of the community in which A and B live. A possesses a considerable supply both of U and V. Parts of the curves are given in Fig. 18 A (i), where the "gold" standard is supposed to be adopted in measuring marginal usefulness and utility. B possesses a little V, but no U, and would be willing (as shown on the curves Fig. 18 B (i.)) to give $\frac{v}{2}$ for u (v and u being small units of V and U), but since u is only worth half as much as v to him, he will not buy it on higher terms than this. Now we have supposed the ratio of utilities of u and v on the relative scale to be 3 : 4. That is to say, if u contains three small units of utility then v contains four. Therefore $\frac{u}{3}$ has the same value-in-exchange or marginal utility as $\frac{v}{4}$, and $\frac{3u}{3}$ or u has the same value-in-exchange as $\frac{3v}{4}$; therefore an offer of $\frac{3v}{4}$, but nothing lower than this, constitutes an "effective" demand for u ; whereas B only offers $\frac{v}{2}$ or $\frac{2v}{4}$ for it. Measuring the intensity of a want by the offer of "gold" it prompts, we should say, that B wants v as much as A does, but wants u less than A does.   This, however, is delusive, for we do not know how much each of them wants the units of "gold" in which all his other wants are estimated.   Suppose we say, "What a man wants he will work for," and ascertain that A would be willing to do half a foot-ton of work for a unit of "gold," whereas B would do one and a half foot-tons for it. This would show that, measured in work, the standard unit was worth three times as much to B as to A.   Reducing the units on the axis of y to $\frac{1}{2}$ for A, and raising them to $\frac{3}{2}$ for B, we shall have the curves of Fig. 18 A (ii) and B (ii) showing the respective "wants" of A and B estimated in willingness to do work.   It will then appear that B wants v three times as much and u twice as much as A does ; but his demand for u is still not effective, for he only offers $\frac{v}{2}$ or $\frac{2v}{4}$ for it, and its exchange-value is $\frac{3v}{4}$.   There is only enough U to supply those who want a unit of it at least as much as they want $\frac{3}{4}$ of a unit of V, and B is not one of these.

Now if A and B had both been obliged to earn their "gold" by work, with equal opportunities, then obviously the unitary marginal utility of "gold," estimated in foot-tons, must have been equally high for both of them, since each would go on getting "gold" till at the margin it was just worth the work it cost to get and no more.   And therefore the marginal utilities of u and v (whether measured in foot-tons or in "gold") must also have stood at the same height for A and B.   Hence B could not have been wholly without U while A possessed it, unless, measured in foot-tons, its marginal usefulness was less to him than to A.

It would remain possible that a foot-ton might represent widely different things to the two men ; but the contention is that this is less probable, and possible only within narrower limits, than in the corresponding case of "gold" under our present system.   I need hardly remind the reader that the assumptions of Fig. 18 are arbitrary, and might have been so made as to yield any result desired.   The figure illustrates a perhaps rational supposition, and throws light on the nature and effects of a change of the standard unit of utility. It does not prove anything as to the actual result which would follow upon any specified change of the standard.

The whole of this note must be regarded as a purely speculative examination of the conditions (whether possible of
approximate realisation or not) under which it might be
roughly true that "what men want most they will pay most
for."

We have now gained a distinct conception of what
is meant by the exchange-value of a commodity.   It is
identical with the marginal utility which a unit of the
commodity has to every member of the community
who possesses it, expressed in terms of the marginal
utility of some concrete unit conventionally agreed
upon.   There is no assignable limit to the divergence
that may exist in the *absolute* utility of the standard
unit at the margin to different members of the community, but the *relative* marginal utilities of the standard
unit and a unit of any other article must be identical to
every member of the community who possesses them, on
the supposition of perfectly developed frictionless exchange, and "small" units.

We may now proceed to show the principle on which
to construct collective or social curves of quantity-
possessed-and-marginal-usefulness without danger of
being misled by the equivocal nature of the standard,
or measure, of usefulness which we shall be obliged to
employ.

In approaching this problem let us take an artificially
simple case, deliberately setting aside all the secondary
considerations and complications that would rise in
practice.

We will suppose, then, that a man has absolute control of a medicinal spring of unique properties, and that
its existence and virtues are generally known to the
medical faculty.   We will further suppose that the
owner is actuated by no consideration except the desire
to make as much as he can out of his property, without
exerting himself to conduct the business of bottling and
disposing of the waters.   He determines, therefore, to
allow people to take the water on whatever terms

prove most profitable to himself, and to concern himself
no further in the matter.

Now there are from time to time men of enormous
wealth who would like to try the water, and would give
many pounds for permission to draw a quart of it, but
these extreme cases fall under no law. One year the
owner might have the offer of £50 for a quart, and for
the next ten years he might never have an offer of more
than £5, and in neither case would there be any regular
flow of demand at these fancy prices. He finds that in
order to strike a broad enough stratum of consumers to
give him a basis for averaging his sales even over a series
of years he must let people draw the water at not more
than ten shillings a quart, at which price he has a small
but appreciable and tolerably steady demand, which he
can average with fair certainty at so much a year. This
means that there is no steady flow of patients to whom
the marginal utility of a quart of the water is greater
than that of ten shillings. In other words, the initial
utility of the water to the community is ten shillings a
quart. Clearly, then, the curve of quantity-and-marginal-
usefulness of the water cuts the axis of y (that is to say,
begins to exist for our purposes) at a value representing
ten shillings a quart. If we were to take our unit on x to
represent a quart and our unit on y to represent a shilling,
then we should have the corresponding values $x = 0, y = 10$.
But since we shall have to deal with large quantities of
the water, it will be convenient to have a larger unit for
diagramatic purposes; and since the rate of 10s. per
quart is also the rate of £5000 per 10,000 quarts, we
may keep our corresponding values $x = 0$, $y = 10$, while
interpreting our unit on x as 10,000 quarts and our unit
on y as £500 (= 10,000 shillings). The curve, then,
cuts the axis of y at the height 10 ; which is to say that
the initial *usefulness* of the water to the community is
£500 per 10,000 quarts, or ten shillings a quart, which
latter estimate being made in "small" units may be
converted into the statement that the initial *utility* of a

quart of the water is equal to that of ten shillings, of
two quarts twenty shillings, etc.*

But at this price customers are few, and the owner
makes only a few pounds a year. He finds that if he
lowers the price the increased consumption more than
compensates him, and as he gradually and experimentally
lowers the price he finds his revenue steadily rising.
Even a reduction to nine shillings enables him to sell

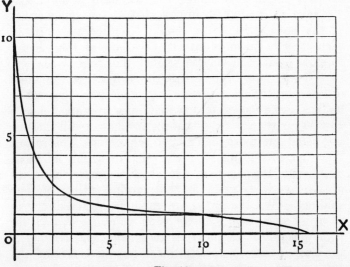

Fig. 19.

about 1000 quarts a year, and so to derive a not incon-
siderable income (£450) from his property. A further
reduction of a shilling about doubles his sale, and he
sells 2000 quarts a year at eight shillings, making £800
income. When he lowers the price still further to six
shillings, he sells between 5000 and 6000 quarts a year,
and his income rises to £1500.

Before following him farther we will look at the prob-

* Whereas it cannot be said that the initial utility of 10,000
quarts is £500, for the initial usefulness is not sustained throughout
the consumption of 10,000 quarts.

lem from the other side. At first no one could get a quart of the water unless its marginal utility to him was as great as that of ten shillings. Now the issue just suffices to supply every one whose marginal want of a quart is as high as six shillings. These and these only possess the water, and on their relative scales it stands as having a marginal utility of six shillings a quart. This, then, may be called the marginal utility of the water *to the community;* only we must bear in mind that we have no reason to suppose that the marginal wants of the possessors are *in themselves* either all equal to each other or all more urgent than those of the yet unsupplied; but relatively to " gold " they will be so.

We will now suppose that the owner tries the effect of lowering the price further still, and finds that when he has come down to four shillings a quart he sells 11,000 quarts a year, so that his revenue is still increasing, being now more than £2200 per annum. This means that over 11,000 quarts are needed to supply all those members of the community to whom the marginal utility of a quart is as great as the marginal utility of four shillings. Still the owner lowers the price, and discovers at every stage *what quantity of the water it is that has the unitary marginal utility to the community corresponding to the price he has fixed.* By this means he is tracing the curve of price-and-quantity-demanded, and he is doing so by giving successive values to y and ascertaining the values of x that severally correspond to them. Fig. 19 shows the supposed result of his experiments, which, however, he will not himself carry on much beyond $y = 1$, which gives $x = 10$,* and represents an income of ten units of area, each unit representing £500, or £5000 in all. The price is now at the rate of £500 per 10,000 quarts, or one shilling per quart, and the annual sales amount to 100,000 quarts. Up to this point we have supposed that every reduction of the price has increased

---

* In the diagram $y = \dfrac{120 - x}{10x + 10} - \dfrac{x^2 - 20x + 100}{50}$.

the total pecuniary yield to the owner. But this cannot go on for ever, inasmuch as the owner is seeking to increase the value of $x \times y$ by diminishing y and increasing x, and since in the nature of the case x cannot be indefinitely extended (there being a limit to the quantity of the water wanted by the public at all) it follows that as y diminishes a point must come at which the increase of x will fail to compensate for the decrease of y, and xy will become smaller as y decreases. This is obvious from the figure. We suppose, then, that when the owner has already reduced his price to one shilling a quart he finds that further reductions fail to bring in a sufficient increase of custom to make up for the decline in price. To make the public take 160,000 quarts a year he would not only have to give it away, but would have to pay something for having it removed.

We have supposed the owner to fix the price and to let the quantity sold fix itself to correspond. That is, we have supposed him to say: Any one on whose relative scale of marginal utilities a quart of this water stands as high as y shillings may have it, and I will see how many quarts per annum it will take to meet the "demand" of all such. Hence he is constructing a curve in which the price is the variable and the quantity demanded at that price is the function. This is a curve of price-and-quantity-demanded. It is usual to call it a "curve of demand" simply, but this is an elliptical, ambiguous, and misleading phrase, which should be strictly excluded from elementary treatises. We have seen (p. 12) that a curve is never a curve of height, time, quantity, utility, or any other *one* thing, but always a curve of connection between some *two* things. The amounts of the things themselves are always represented by straight lines, and it is the connection of the corresponding pairs of these lines that is depicted on the curve. If we not only always bear this in mind, but always express it, it will be an inestimable safeguard against confusion and ambiguity, and we may make it a convention always to put the magnitude which we regard as the variable first. Thus the curve we have just traced is a curve of price-and-quantity-demanded.

But it would have been just as easy to suppose our owner to fix the quantity issued, and then let the price fix itself. The curve itself would, of course, be the same (compare pp. 3, 13), but we should now regard it as a curve of quantity-issued-and-intensity-of-demand. The price obtainable always indicating the intensity of the demand for more when just so much is issued. From this point of view also it might be called a "curve of demand," but "demand" would then mean intensity of demand (the quantity issued being given), and would be measured by the price or y. In the other case "demand" would mean quantity demanded (at a given price), and would be measured by x.

Now this curve of quantity-issued-and-intensity-of-demand is the same thing as the curve of quantity-possessed-(by the community)-and-marginal-usefulness, or briefly quantity-and-price. Thus if we call the curve a curve of price-and-quantity we indicate that we are supposing the owner to fix the price and let the quantity sold fix itself, whereas if we call it the curve of quantity-and-price we are supposing the owner to fix the amount he will issue and let the price fix itself. In either case we put the variable first, and call it the curve of the variable-and-function.

Regarding the curve as one of quantity-and-price then, we suppose the owner to say : I will draw x times 10,000 quarts (of course x may be a fraction) from my spring every year, and will see how urgent in comparison with the want of "gold" the want that the last quart meets turns out to be. In this case it is obvious that as the owner increases the issue the new wants satisfied by the larger supply will be less urgent, relatively to "gold," than the wants supplied before, but still the marginal utility of a quart relatively to "gold" will be the same to all the purchasers, and will be greater to them than to any of those who do not yet take any. Thus as the issue increases the marginal utility to the community of a quart steadily sinks on the relative scale of the community, and shows itself, as in the case of the individual, to be a decreasing function of the quantity possessed, each fresh increment meeting a less urgent want than the last. But meanwhile the *total* service done to the community by the water is increased by every additional quart. The man who bought one quart a year for ten shillings, and who buys two quarts a year when it comes down to eight shillings, and ten quarts a year when it is only a shilling, would still be willing to give ten shillings for a single quart if he could not get it cheaper, and the second and following quarts, though not ministering to so urgent a want as the first, yet in no way interfere with or lessen the advantage it has already conferred, while they add a further advantage of their own. Thus from his first quart the man now gets for a shilling the full advantage which he estimated at ten shillings, and from the second quart the advantage he estimated at eight shillings, and so on. It is only the last quart from which he derives an advantage no more than equivalent to what he gives for it. We may, therefore, still preserving the "gold" standard, say that the total utility of the q quarts which A consumes in the year is made up of the whole sum he would have given for one quart rather than have none, *plus* the whole quantity he would have given for a second quart sooner than have only one + . . . + the whole sum he gives for the qth quart sooner than be satisfied with $(q-1)$. In like manner the successive quarts, up to p, which B adds to his yearly consumption as the price comes down, each confers a fresh benefit, while leaving the benefits already conferred by the others as great as ever. Thus we should construct for A, B, C, etc., severally, curves of quantity-and-total-utility of the water, on which we could read the total benefit derived from any given quantity of the water by each individual measured in terms of the marginal utility to him of the unit of gold. And regarding the total utility as a function of the quantity possessed, we shall, of course, find that each consumer goes on possessing himself of more till the first derived function (rate at which more is adding to his satisfaction) coincides with the price at which he can purchase the water.

In like manner we may, if we choose, add up all the utilities of the successive quarts to *A*, *B*, *C*, etc., measured in "gold," as they accrue (neglecting the fact that they are not subjectively but only objectively commensurate with each other), and may make a curve showing the grand total of the utility to the community of the whole quantity of water consumed. And this curve would of course continue to rise (though at a decreasing rate) as long as any one who had anything to give in exchange wanted a quart more of the water than he had.

Thus we have seen that as the issue increases the utility of a quart at the margin to each individual and to the whole community continuously falls on the relative scale, the exchange value of course (recorded in the price) steadily accompanying it ; while at the same time each extra quart confers a fresh advantage on the community without in any way interfering with or lessening the advantages already conferred ; that is to say, the total advantage to the community increases as the issue increases, whereas the marginal usefulness constantly decreases. The maximum total utility would be realised when the issue became free, and every one was allowed as much of the water as he wanted, and then the marginal utility would sink to nothing, that is to say, no one would attach any value to more than he already had. This is in precise accordance with the results already obtained with reference to a single individual. The total effect is at its maximum when the marginal effectiveness is zero.

But now returning to the owner of the spring, we note that his attention is fixed neither upon the total nor the marginal utility of the water, but on the total price he receives, and we note that that price is represented in the diagram by a rectangle, the base of which is *x*, or the quantity sold measured in the unit agreed upon, and the height *y*, the price or rate per unit (determined by its marginal usefulness) at which when issued in that quantity the commodity sells. The area, therefore, is *xy*. And this brings us to the important principle involved in what is known as the "law of indifference." By this law the owner finds himself obliged to sell *all* his wares at the price which *the least urgently needed* will fetch, for he cannot as a rule make a separate bargain with each customer for each unit, making each pay as much for each successive unit as that unit is worth to him ; since, unless he sold the same quantity at the same price to all his customers, those whom he charged high would deal with those whom he charged low, instead of directly with him. "There cannot be two prices for the same article in the same market." Thus we see again, and see with ever increasing distinctness, that the exchange value of a commodity is regulated by its marginal utility, and is independent of the service which that particular specimen happens to render to the particular individual who purchases it.

Thus (if we bear in mind the purely relative and therefore socially equivocal nature of our standard of utility) we may now generalise the conclusions we reached in the first instance with exclusive reference to the individual. From the collective as from the individual point of view the marginal utility of a commodity is a function of the quantity of it possessed or commanded. If the quantity changes, the communal marginal utility and therefore the exchange-value changes with it ; and this altogether irrespective of the nature of the causes which produce the change in quantity. Whether it is that nature provides so much and no more, or that some one who has power to control the supply chooses, for whatever reason, to issue just so much and no more, or that producers think it worth while to produce so much and no more—all this, though of the utmost consequence in determining whether and how the supply can be further changed, is absolutely immaterial in the primary determination of the marginal utility, and therefore of the exchange-value, so long as just so much and no more *is* issued. This amount is the variable, and, given a relation between the variable and the function (*i.e.* given the curve), then, when the variable is determined, no matter how, why, or by whom, the function is thereby determined also (compare p. 62).

Exchange value, then, is relative marginal value-in-use, and is a function of quantity possessed.

The " Law of Indifference " is of fundamental importance in economics. Its full significance and bearing cannot be grasped till the whole field of economics has been traversed ; but we may derive both amusement and instruction, at the stage we have now reached, from the consideration of the various attempts which are made to evade it, and from the light which a reference to it throws upon the real nature of many familiar transactions.

In the first place, then, sale by auction is often an attempt to escape the law of indifference. The auctioneer has, say, ten pictures by a certain master whose work does not often come into the market, and his skill consists in getting the man who is most keen for a specimen to give his full price for the first sold. Then he has to let the second go cheaper, because the keenest bidder is no longer competing ; but he tries to make the next man give *his* outside price ; and so on. The bidders, on the other hand, if cool enough, try to form a rough estimate of the *marginal* utility of the pictures, that is to say, of the price which the tenth man will give for a picture when the nine keenest bidders are disposed of, and they know that if they steadily refuse to go above this point there will be one for each of them at the price. When the

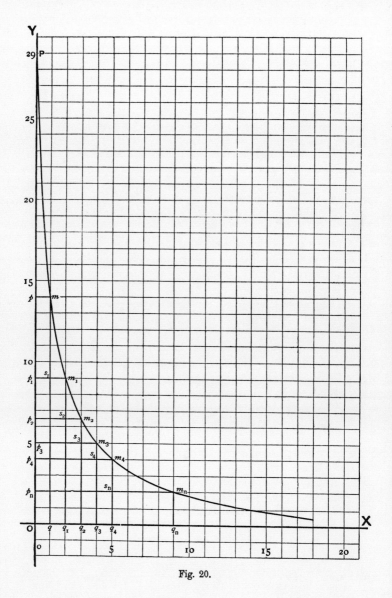

Fig. 20.

To face page 103.

II   STOCKBROKING   103

things on sale are such as can be readily got elsewhere, the auctioneer is powerless to evade the law of indifference.

Another instance constantly occurs in the stock markets. A broker wishes to dispose of a large amount of a certain stock, which is being taken, say, at 95. But he knows that only a little can be sold at that price, because a few thousands would be enough to meet all demands of the urgency represented by that figure. In fact, the stock he has to part with would suffice to meet all the wants represented by 93 and upwards, and accordingly the law of indifference would compel him to part with the first thousand at that rate just as much as the last if he were to offer all he means to sell at once. This, in fact, will be the selling price of the whole when he has completed his operations. But meanwhile he endeavours to hold the law of indifference at bay by producing only a small part of his stock and doing business at 95 till there are no more demands urgent enough to prompt an offer of more than $94\frac{7}{8}$. He then proceeds cautiously to meet these wants likewise, obtaining in each case the maximum that the other party is willing to give ; and so on, till, if completely successful, he has let the stock down $\frac{1}{8}$ at a time from 95 to 93. By this time, of course, not only his own last batch, but all the others that he has sold, are down at 93. The law of indifference has been defeated only so far as he is concerned, and not in its general operation on the market.

The general principle involved is illustrated, without special reference to the cases cited, in Fig. 20. The law of indifference dictates that if the quantity Oq_4 is to be sold, then $Oq, qq_1, q_1q_2, q_2q_3, q_3q_4$ must all be treated indifferently, and therefore sold at the price measured by Op_4 ($=q_4m_4$). This would realise an amount represented by the area p_4q_4. But the seller endeavours to mask the fact that Oq_4 is to be sold, and by issuing separate instalments tries to secure the successive areas $pq + s_1q_1 + s_2q_2 + s_3q_3 + s_4q_4$. Obviously the "limit" of this process, under the most favourable possible circumstances, is the securing of the whole area bounded by the curve, the axes, and the line q_nm_n (where q_n stands for the last of the series q, q_1, etc.)* If the law of indifference takes

---

* If Op or q^m is $f(Oq)$, i.e. if y is $f(x)$, then the area in question will be $\int_0^x f(x)dx$ (see pp. 23, 31). The meaning of this symbol may

full effect the seller is apt to regard the area Pp_nm_n as a territory to be reclaimed. The public, he thinks, has got it without paying for it. If the law of indifference is completely evaded, the public, in its turn, is apt to think that it has been cheated to the extent of this area.

We may now consider some more special cases of attempts to escape the action of the law of indifference. The system of " two prices " in retail dealing is a good instance. It is an attempt to isolate two classes of customers and to confine the action of the law of indifference to equalising the prices within these classes, taken severally. In fact, the principle of "fixed prices in retail trade " is strictly involved in the frank acceptance of the law of indifference ; and all evasions or modifications of that principle are attempts to escape the action of the law. The extent to which " double prices " prevail in London is perhaps not generally realised. A differential charge of a halfpenny or penny a quart on milk, for instance, according to the average status (estimated by house rent) of

---

now be explained. The sum of all the rectangular areas is $pq + s_1q_1 + s_2q_2 +$ etc., or $qm \cdot Oq + q_1m_1 \cdot qq_1 + q_2m_2 \cdot q_1q_2 +$ etc., but qm is $f(Oq)$, q_1m_1 is $f(Oq_1)$, q_2m_2 is $f(Oq_2)$, etc. Therefore the sum of the areas is

$$f(Oq) \cdot Oq + f(Oq_1) \cdot qq_1 + f(Oq_2) \cdot q_1q_2 + \text{etc.}$$

But $Oq = qq_1 = q_1q_2 =$ etc. We may call this quantity "the increment of x," and may write it Δx. The sum of the rectangular areas will then be

$$\{f(Oq) + f(Oq_1) + f(Oq_2) + \text{etc.}\} \ \Delta x,$$
$$\text{or sum } \{f(Oq)\} \ \Delta x, \text{ or } \Sigma \{f(Oq)\} \ \Delta x.$$

When we wish to indicate the limit of any expression into which Δx, *i.e.* an increment of x, enters, as the increment becomes smaller and smaller, it is usual to say that Δx becomes dx. In the limit then $\Sigma \{f(Oq)\} \Delta x$ becomes $\int f(Oq)dx$, where $\int$ is simply the letter s, the abbreviation of "sum." The symbol then means, the limit of the sum of the areas of the rectangles as the bases become smaller and the number of the rectangles greater. But we have further to indicate the limits within which we are to perform this summing of the rectangles. If we wished to express the area $q_1m_1m_3q_3$ the limits would be Oq_1 and Oq_3. We should wish to sum all the rectangles bounded by $f(Oq_1)$, *i.e.* q_1m_1, and $f(Oq_3)$, *i.e.* q_3m_3. This we should indicate thus—

$$\int_{Oq_1}^{Oq_3} f(Oq) \cdot dx$$

the inhabitants of each street or neighbourhood, seems to be common.

It is clear, too, that when he has established a system of differential charges, the tradesman can, if he likes, sell to the low-priced customer at a price which would not pay him* if charged all round ; for the small profit he would make on each transaction would not enable him to meet his standing expenses. Having met them, however, from the profits of his high-priced business, he may now put down any balance of receipts over expenses out of pocket on the other business as pure gain. If in Fig. 20 the rectangles represent not the actual receipts for the respective sales, but the balance of receipts over expenses out of pocket on each several transaction, we may suppose that the dealer requires to realise an area of 20 in order to meet his standing expenses and make a living. He can do business to the extent of Oq_4 at the (gross)† rate of profit Op_4, which gives him his area of 20, i.e. p_4q_4. If he did business to the extent of Oq_n at a uniform (gross) profit of Op_n, he would only secure an area of 18, i.e. p_nq_n, and so could not carry on business at all. But if he can keep Oq_4 at the profit Op_4, and

---

And the area OPm_nq_n will be

$$\int_0^{Oq_n} f(Oq)\,.\,dx$$

This means that the values successively assumed by Oq in the expression, sum $(Oq\,.\,dx)$ are, respectively, all the values between Oq_1 and Oq_3, or all the values between 0 and Oq_n. Finally, since the successive values of Oq are the successive values of x, and since Oq_n is the last value of x we are to consider, we may write the expression for OPm_nq_n

$$\int_0^c f(x)\,.\,dx$$

or the expression for $q_1m_1m_nq_n$

$$\int_{q_1m_1}^x f(x)\,.\,dx$$

remembering the x in $f(x)$ stands for all the successive values of the variable, x, whereas in $\int_0^x$ or $\int_{q_1m_1}^x$ or generally $\int_{constant}^x$ x stands only for the *last* of the values of the variable considered.

* This phrase is used in anticipation, but is perhaps sufficiently clear (see below).

† I.e. surplus of receipts over expenses out of pocket *on that transaction*, all standing expenses being already incurred.

then without detriment to the other add $q_4 q_n$ at a profit Op_n, he secures $20 + 8$, *i.e.* $p_4 q_4 + s_n q_n$. Nay, it is conceivable enough that he could not carry on business at all except on the principle of double prices. Suppose, in the case illustrated by the figure, that he must realise an area of 25 in order to go on. It will be found that no rectangle containing so large an area can be drawn in the curve. The maximum rectangle will be found to correspond to the value of nearly 4·5 for x, which will give an area of only a little more than 20. If the law of indifference, then, takes full effect, our tradesman cannot do business at all ; but if he can deal with Oq_4 and $q_4 q_n$ separately, he may do very well.

In this case the " double price " system is the only possible one ; and the high-priced customers are not really paying an unnaturally high price. For unless *some one* pays as high as that the ware cannot be brought into the market at all. But it would be easy so to modify our supposition as to make the tradesman a kind of commercial Robin Hood, forcing up the price for one class of customers above the level at which they would naturally be able to obtain their goods, and then lowering it for others below the paying line.

The differential charges of railway companies illustrate this. A company finds that certain goods Oq must necessarily be sent on their line, whereas qq_4 may be equally well sent by another line. An average surplus of receipts over expenses out of pocket represented by an area of four units per unit of x will pay the company; *i.e.* Op_4 per unit, giving $p_4 q_4$ or 20 on the carriage of Oq_4 would pay. On Oq the company puts a charge which will yield gross profits at the rate of Op, and thus secure $pq = 14$. They then underbid the other company for the carriage of qq_4. Op_4 being the minimum average gross profit that will pay (in view of standing expenses), they offer to carry at a gross profit of Op_n, for their standing expenses are already incurred, and they thus secure an extra gross profit of qs_n ($= 8$) which, together with the pq ($= 14$) they have already secured, gives them a total of 22, or 2 more than if they had run at uniform prices. Of the ten extra units of area which they extracted from the consigners of Oq, they have given eight to the consigners of qq_4 in the shape of a deduction from the legitimate charge.

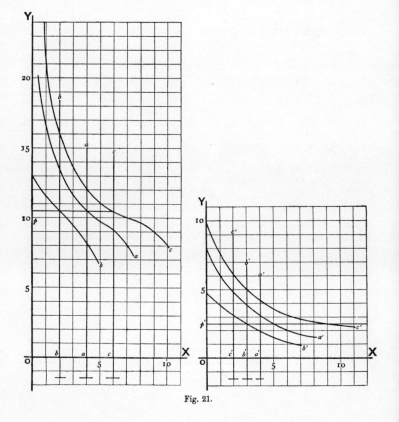

Fig. 21.

To face page 107.

Another interesting case is that of a theatre.   Here the
"two (or more) price" system is disguised by withholding
from the low-price customers certain conveniences which practically cost nothing, but which serve as a badge of distinction
and enable the high-price customers to pay for the privilege
of being separated from the rest without offensively parading
before them that this separation is in fact the privilege for
which they are paying 8s. each.   The accommodation is
limited, and the nature of the demand varies according to the
popularity of the piece.   Except under quite exceptional circumstances custom fixes the charges for stalls and pit, to which we
will confine ourselves ; and though the manager would rather
fill his floor with stalls than with benches, yet he is glad of all
the half-crowns which do not displace half-guineas, since his
expenses out of pocket for each additional pittite are trivial or
non-existent.   Neglecting the difference of space assigned to
a sitter in a stall and on a bench, let us suppose the whole
floor to hold 800 seats, 400 of which are made into stalls.
Representing a hundred theatre-goers by a unit on x, and the
rate of 1s. a head, or £5 a 100 by the unit on y, and so
making each unit of area represent £5 receipts, we may
read the two curves a and a' in Fig. 21 thus.   There is a
nightly supply of four hundred theatre-goers who value the
entertainment, accompanied by the dignity and comfort of a
stall at not less than 10s. 6d. a seat (rate of £52 : 10s. per
hundred seats.)   There are also five hundred more who value
it, with the discomforts of the pit, at 2s. 6d. a seat (rate of
£12 : 10s. per hundred).   There is not accommodation for all
the latter, since there are but four hundred pit seats, and
custom prevents the manager from filling his pit at a little
over 3s. a place as he might do.   So he lets his customers fight
it out at the door and takes in four hundred at 2s. 6d. each
(area $p'a'$).   His takings are $(10\cdot5 \times 4 + 2\cdot5 \times 4)$ times £5 =
£260, since each unit of area represents £5.   The areas
are pa and $p'a'$.   The former pa is as great as the marginal utility of the article offered admits of, but the latter
$p'a'$ is limited horizontally by the space available and vertically by custom.

As the public gets tired of the play the curves a and a' are
replaced by b and b'.   The manager might fill his stalls by
going down to 8s., and might almost fill his pit at 2s.   But

custom forbids this. His prices are fixed and his issue of tickets fixes itself. He has 200 stalls and 300 places in the pit taken every night. Area $= pb + p'b'$. Receipts $(10\cdot5 \times 2 + 2\cdot5 \times 3)$ times £5 = £142 : 10s.

When the manager puts on a new piece the curves c and c' replace b and b'; and finding that he can issue six hundred stall tickets per night at 10s. 6d., the manager pushes his stalls back and cuts down the pit to two hundred places, for which six or seven hundred theatre-goers fight; several hundred more, who would gladly have paid 2s. 6d. each for places, retreating when they find that they must wait a few hours and fight with wild beasts for ten minutes in addition to paying their half-crowns. When the two hundred successful competitors find that the manager has not sacrificed £80 a night for the sake of keeping the four hundred seats they consider due to them and their order, they try to convince him that a pittite and peace therewith is better than a stalled ox and contention with it. It would be interesting to know in what terms they would state their case ; but evidently the merely commercial principles of " business " do not command their loyal assent. The areas $pc + p'c'$ are $(10\cdot5 \times 6 + 2\cdot5 \times 2)$ times £5 = £340.

The case of " reduced terms " at boarding schools is very like the cases of the railway and the theatre. The reader may work it out in detail. As long as the school is not full, the " reduced " pupils do something towards helping things along, if they pay anything more than they actually eat and break. At the same time it would be impossible to meet the standing expenses and carry on the school if the terms were reduced all round. If pupils are taken at reduced terms when their places could be filled by paying ones, then the master is sacrificing the full amount of the reduction.

These instances, which might be increased almost indefinitely, will serve to illustrate the importance of the law of indifference and the attempts to escape its action.

Having now a sufficiently clear and precise conception of the marginal utilities of various commodities *to the community*, we may take up again from the general point of view the investigation which we have already

entered upon (on p. 58) with reference to the individual,
and may inquire what principles will regulate the direction taken in an industrial community by the labour
(and other efforts or sacrifices, if there are any others)
needful to production.

Strictly speaking, this does not come within the
scope of our present inquiry. We have already seen
that the exchange value of an article is a function of the
quantity possessed, completely independent of the way
in which that quantity comes to be possessed ; and
any inquiries as to the circumstances that determine, in
particular cases, the actual quantity produced and therefore possessed, fall into the domain of the "theory of
production" or "making" rather than into that of the
"theory of value" or "worth." But the two subjects
have been so much confounded, and the connection
between them is in reality so intimate and so important,
that even an elementary treatment of the subject of
"value" would be incomplete unless it included an
examination of the simplest case of connection between
value and what is called cost of production. The consideration of any case except the simplest would be out
of place here.

Suppose A can command the efforts and sacrifices
needed to produce either U or V, and suppose the production of either will require the same application of
these productive agents per unit produced. Obviously
A, if he approaches his problem from the purely mercantile side, has simply to ask, "Which of the two, when
produced, will be worth most in 'gold' to the community ?" i.e., he must inquire which of the two has the
highest relative marginal utility, or stands highest on the
relative scale. Suppose a unit u has, at the margin,
twice the relative utility of the unit v ; A will then
devote himself to the production of U, for by so doing
he will create a thing having twice the exchange value,
and will therefore obtain twice as much in exchange, as
if he took the other course. He will therefore produce

u simply because, when produced, it will exchange for more "gold" than v. A will not be alone in this preference. Other producers, whose productive forces are freely disposable, will likewise produce U in preference to V, and the result will be a continual increase in the quantity of U. Now we have seen that an increased quantity of U means a decreased marginal usefulness of U measured in "gold," so that the production of U in greater and greater quantities means the gradual declension on the relative scale of its unitary marginal utility, and its gradual approximation to that of V, which will cause the exchange values of u and v to become more and more nearly equal. But as long as the marginal utility of u stands at all above that of v on the relative scale, the producers will still devote themselves by preference to the production of U, and consequently its marginal usefulness will continue to fall on the scale until at last it comes down to that of V. Then the marginal utilities and exchange values of u and v will be equal, and as the expenditure of productive forces necessary to make them is by hypothesis equal also, there will be no reason why producers should prefer the one to the other. There will now be equilibrium, and if more of *either* is produced, then more of *both* will be produced in such proportions as to preserve the equilibrium now established. In fact the diagram (Fig. 14, p. 60) by which we illustrated the principle upon which a wise man would distribute his own personal labour between two methods of directly supplying his own wants, will apply without modification to the principles upon which purely mercantile considerations tend to distribute the productive forces in a mercantile society. But though the diagram is the same there is a momentous difference in its signification, for in the one case it represents a genuine balancing of desire against desire in one and the same mind or "subject," where the several desires have a real common measure ; in the other case it represents a mere mechanical and external equivalence in the desires gratified arrived at by measuring each of them in the corresponding desires for "gold" existing respectively in *different* "*subjects*."

It only remains to generalise our conclusions. No new principle is introduced by supposing an indefinite number of alternatives, instead of only two, to lie before the wielders of productive forces. There will always be a tendency to turn all freely disposable productive forces towards those branches of production in which the smallest sum of labour and other necessaries will produce a given utility ; that is to say, to the production of those commodities which have the highest marginal utility in proportion to the labour, etc., required to produce them ; and this rush of productive forces into these particular channels will increase the amount of the respective commodities, and so reduce their marginal usefulness till units of them are no longer of more value at the margin than units of other things that can be made by the same expenditure of productive forces. There will then no longer be any special reason for further increasing the supply of them.

The productive forces of the community then, like the labour of a self-sufficing industrial unit, will tend to distribute themselves in such a way that a given sum of productive force will produce equal utilities at the margin (measured externally by equivalents in " gold ") wherever applied.

To make this still clearer, we may take a single case in detail, and supposing general equilibrium to exist amongst the industries, may ask what will regulate the extent to which a newly developed industry will be taken up ? But as a preliminary to this inquiry we must define more closely our idea of a general equilibrium amongst the industries. On p. 73 *sqq* we established the principle that if commodities A and B are freely exchanged, and commodities B and C are freely exchanged also, then the unitary marginal utilities, and thus the exchange values of a and c, may be expressed

each in terms of the other, even though it should happen
that no owners of A want C, and no owners of C want A,
and in consequence there is no direct exchange between
them.   In like manner the principle of the distribution
of efforts and sacrifices just established enables us to
select a single industry as a standard and bring all the
others into comparison with it.   It will be convenient,
as we took gold for our standard commodity, so to take
gold-digging as our standard industry ; and as we have
written " gold " as a short expression for " gold and all the
commodities in the circle of exchange, expressed in terms
of gold," so we may write " gold-digging " as a short expression for " gold-digging and all the industries open to
producers, in equilibrium with gold-digging," and we
shall mean by one industry being in equilibrium with
another that the conditions are such that a unit of
effort-and-sacrifice applied at the margin of either
industry will produce an equivalent utility.*   If, then,
a sufficient number of persons have a practical option
between gold-digging (α) and cattle-breeding (β), this
will establish equilibrium between these two occupations
α and β, in accordance with the principle just laid
down ; and if a sufficient number of other persons to
whom gold-digging is impossible have a practical option
between cattle-breeding (β) and corn-growing (γ), then
that will establish equilibrium between β and γ.   But
since there will always be equilibrium between α and β
as long as sufficient persons have the option between
them, and since that equilibrium will be restored, when-
ever disturbed, by the forces that first established it, it
follows that if there is equilibrium between β and γ

* To speak of the "margin" of an industry again involves an
anticipation of matters not dealt with in this volume, but I trust it
will create no confusion.   It must be taken here simply to mean " a
unit of productive force added to those already employed in a certain
industry," and the assumption is that all units are employed at the
same advantage, the difference in the utility of their yields being due
simply to the decreasing marginal utility of the same unit of the com
modity as the quantity of the commodity progressively increases.

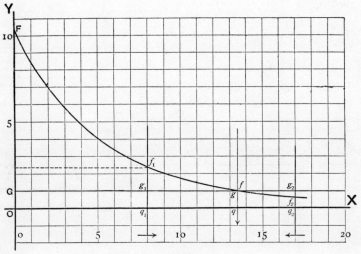

Fig. 22.

To face page 113.

there will be equilibrium between a and γ also. We may therefore conveniently select a or gold-digging as the industry of general reference, and may say that a man will prefer γ or corn-growing to "gold-digging" as long as the yield is higher in the former industry, although as a matter of fact it is not the yield in gold-digging but the yield in cattle-breeding (itself equilibrated with gold-digging) with which he directly compares his results in corn growing. Industries in equilibrium with the same are in equilibrium with each other.

We assume, then, that there is a point of equilibrium about which all the industries, librated with each other directly and indirectly, oscillate ; and, neglecting the oscillations, we use the yield to a given application of productive forces in gold-digging as the representative of the equivalent yield in all the other industries in equilibrium with it.

Now we imagine a new industry to be proposed, and producers who command freely disposable efforts and sacrifices to turn their attention to it. Their option is between the new industry and "gold-digging," in the extended sense just explained. We are justified in assuming, for the sake of simplicity, that the whole sum of the productive forces under consideration would not sensibly affect the marginal usefulness of " gold " (in the extended sense, observe) if applied to " gold-digging ;" that is to say, we assume that in no case will the new industry draw to itself so great a volume of effort-and-sacrifice as to starve the other industries of the world, taken collectively, and make the general want of the things they yield perceptibly more keen. Therefore, in examining the alternative of " gold-digging," we assume that the whole volume of labour and other requisites of production, or effort-and sacrifice, which is in question might be applied to " gold-digging " without reducing the marginal usefulness of " gold," or might be withdrawn from it without increasing that usefulness. The yield in "gold" of any quantity of labour and other requisites, then, would be exactly proportional to that quantity.

Fixing on any arbitrary unit of effort-and-sacrifice (say 100,000 foot-tons), and taking as our standard unit of utility the gold that it would produce (say 30 ounces), we may represent the "gold" yield of any given amount of labour and other requisites by the aid of a straight line, drawn parallel to the abscissa at a distance of unity from it (Fig. 22). Thus if O*q* effort and sacrifice were devoted to "gold-digging," the area G*q* would represent the exchange value of the result. Now let the upper curve on the figure be the curve of quantity-and-marginal-usefulness of the new product, the unit of quantity being that amount which the unit of labour and other requisites (100,000 foot-tons) will produce. And here we must make a simplification which would be violent if we were studying the theory of production, but which is perfectly legitimate for our present purpose. We must suppose, namely, that however much or little of the new product is secured it is always got under the same conditions, so that the yield per unit effort-and-sacrifice is the same at every stage of the process. But though the *quantity* produced by a unit of productive force is always the same its marginal usefulness and exchange value will of course descend, according to the universal law, as the total quantity of the ware increases. In the first instance, then, the commercial mind has simply to ask, "Are there persons to whom such an amount of this article as I can produce by applying the unit of productive force will be worth more than the 'gold' I could produce by the same application of force?" In other words, "Will the unit of productive force applied to this industry produce more than the unit of utility?" Under the conditions represented in the figure the answer will be a decisive affirmative, and the producer will turn his disposable forces of production into the new channel. But as soon as he does so the most importunate demands for the new article will be satisfied, and if any further production is carried on it must be to meet a demand of decreasing importunacy, *i.e.* the marginal utility of the article is decreasing, and the exchange value of the yield of the unit of productive force in the new industry is falling. Production will continue, however, as long as there is any advantage in the new industry over gold-production, *i.e.* till the yield of unit productive force in the new industry has sunk to unit utility.

Thus, if Oq_1 effort and sacrifice is devoted to the new industry, the marginal usefulness of the product will be measured by q_1f_1, and the exchange value of the whole output by the rectangle bounded by the dotted line and q_1f_1, etc. This is much more than Gq_1 the alternative " gold " yield to the same productive force. But there is still an advantage in devoting productive forces to the new industry, since q_1f_1 is greater than q_1g_1, and even if the present producers are unable to devote more work to it, or unwilling to do so, because it would diminish the area of the rectangle (p. 96), yet there will be others anxious to get a return to their work at the rate of q_1f_1 instead of q_1g_1. Obviously, then, the new commodity will be produced to the extent of Oq where $qf = qg$, *i.e.*, the point at which the curve cuts the straight line Gg, which is the alternative " gold " curve. If production be carried farther it will be carried on at a disadvantage. At q_2, for instance, q_2f_2 is less than q_2g_2, that is to say, if the supply is already Oq_2, then a further supply will meet a demand the importunity of which is less than that of the demand for the " gold " which the same productive force would yield. This will beget a tendency to desert the industry, and will reduce the quantity towards Oq.

We have supposed our units of " gold " and the new commodity so selected that it requires equal applications of productive agencies to secure either, but in practice we usually estimate commodities in customary units that have no reference to any such equivalence. This of course does not affect our reasoning. If the unit of F is such that our unit of labour and other necessaries yields a hundred units of F and only one unit of G, then, obviously, we shall go on producing F until, but only until, the exchange value of a hundred units of F (the product of unit of labour, etc., in F) becomes equal to the exchange value of one unit of G (the product of unit of labour, etc., in G). Or, generally, if it needs x times as much effort and sacrifice to produce one unit A as it takes to produce one unit B, then it takes as much to produce x units B as to produce one unit A, and there will always be an advantage either in producing xb or in producing one a, by preference, unless the exchange value of both is the same; that is to say, unless the marginal value of a equals x times that of b. Thus, *if a contains x times as much work as b, then there will not be equilibrium until A and B are produced in such amounts as to make the exchange value of a just x times the exchange value of b.*

This, then, is the connection between the exchange value of an article (that can be produced freely and in indefinite quantities) and the amount of work it contains. Here as everywhere the quantity possessed determines the marginal utility, and with it the exchange value; and if the curve is given us we have only to look at the quantity-index in order to read the exchange value of the commodity (see pp. 62, 67). But in the practically and theoretically very important case of commodities freely producible in indefinite quantities we may now note this further fact as to the principle by which the position of the quantity-index is in its turn fixed—that fluid labour-and-sacrifice tends so to distribute itself and so to shift the quantity-indexes as to make *the unitary marginal utility of every commodity directly proportional to the amount of work it contains.*

This fact, that the effort-and-sacrifice needed to produce two articles is, in a large class of cases (those, namely, in which production is free and capable of indefinite extension), proportional to the exchange values of the articles themselves, has led to a strange and persistent delusion not only amongst the thoughtless and ignorant but amongst many patient and earnest thinkers, who have not realised that the exchange value of a commodity is a function of the quantity possessed, and may be made to vary indefinitely by regulating that quantity. The delusion to which I refer is that it is the amount of effort-and-sacrifice or "labour" needed to produce a commodity which *gives that commodity its value in exchange.* A glance at Fig. 22 will remind the reader of the magnitude and scope of the error involved in this idea. The commodity, on our hypothesis, always contains the same amount of effort-and-sacrifice per unit, whether much or little is produced, but the fact that only the unit of "labour" has been put into it does not prevent its exchange value being more than unity all the time till it exists in the quantity Oq, nor does the fact of its containing a full unit of labour keep its exchange value up to unity as soon as it exists in excess of the quantity Oq. What gives the commodity its value in exchange is the quantity in which it exists and the nature of the curve connecting quantity and marginal usefulness ; and it is no more true and no more sensible to say that the quantity of "labour" contained in an article determines its value than it would be to say that it is the amount of money which I give for a thing that makes it useful or beautiful. The fact is, of course, precisely the other way. I give so much money for the thing because I expect to find it useful or think it beautiful ; and the producer puts so much "labour" into the making of a thing because when made he expects it to have such and such an exchange value. Thus one thing is not worth twice as much as another because it has twice as much "labour" in it, but producers have been willing to put twice as much "labour" into it because they know that when produced it will be worth twice as much, because it will be twice as "useful" or twice as much desired.

This is so obvious that serious thinkers could not have fallen into and persisted in the error, and would not be perpetually liable to relapse into it, were it not for certain considerations which must now be noticed.

In the first place, if we have not fully realised and completely assimilated the fact that exchange value is a function of the quantity possessed, and changes as the quantity-index shifts, it seems reasonable to say, "It is all very well to say that because people want *a* twice as much as *b* they will be *willing to do* twice as much to get *a* as they will to get *b*, but how does it follow that they will be *able to get* the article *a* by devoting just twice as much labour to it as to *b*? Surely you cannot maintain that it *always happens* that the thing people want twice as much needs exactly twice as much "labour" to produce as the other? And yet you admit yourself that the thing which has twice the exchange value always does contain twice the "labour." If it is not a chance, then, what is it?" The answer is obvious, and the reader is recommended to write it out for himself as clearly and concisely as possible, and then to compare it with the following statement: If people want *a* just twice as much as *b*, and no more, it does not follow that a producer will find *a* just twice as hard to get, but it does follow that if he finds *a* is *more* than twice as hard to get (say *x* times as hard) he will not get it at all, but will devote his productive energies to making *b*. Confining ourselves, for the sake of simplicity, to these two commodities, we note that other producers will, for the like reason, also produce B in preference to A. The result will be an increased supply of B, and, therefore, a decreased intensity of the want of it; whereas the want of A remaining the same as it was, the utility of *a* is now more than twice as great as the (diminished) utility of *b*; and as soon as the want of *b* relatively to the want of *a* has sunk to $\frac{1}{x}$, then one *a* is worth *x* *b*'s, and as it needs just *x* times the effort-and-sacrifice to produce *a*, there is now equilibrium, and A and B will *both* be made in such quantities as to preserve the equilibrium henceforth; but the proportion of one utility to the other, and the proportion of the "labour" contained in one commodity to that contained in the other, do not "happen" to coincide; they have been *made* to coincide by a suitable adjustment of efforts so as to secure the maximum satisfaction.

Another source of confusion lurks in the ambiguous use of the word "because"; and behind that in a loose conception of what is implied and what is involved in one thing being the " cause " of another.

Thus we sometimes say " x is true because y is true," when we mean not that y being true is the *cause*, but that it is the *evidence* of x being true.   For instance, we might say "prime beef is less esteemed by the public than prime mutton, because the latter sells at 1d. or ½d. more per pound than the former."   By this we should mean to indicate the higher price given for mutton not as the cause of its being more esteemed, but as the evidence that it is so.*   So again, "Is the House sitting?"—"Yes! because the light on the clock-tower is shining."   This does not mean that the light shining causes the House to sit, but that it shows us it is sitting.

In like manner a man may say, " If I want to know how much the exchange value of a exceeds that of b, I shall look into the cost of producing them, and if I find four times as much ' labour ' put into a, I shall say a is worth four times b, because I find that producers have put four times the ' labour ' into it ; " and if he means by this that he knows the respective values in exchange of a and b on the evidence of the amount of effort-and-sacrifice which he finds producers willing to put into them respectively, then we have no fault to find with his economics, though he is using language dangerously liable to misconception.   But if he means that it is the effort-and-sacrifice, or "labour," contained in them which *gives* them their value in exchange, he is entirely wrong.   As a matter of fact, the defenders of the erroneous theory sometimes make the assertion in the erroneous sense, victoriously defend it, when pressed, in the true sense, and then retain and apply it in the erroneous sense.

Again, though it is never true that the quantity of "labour" contained in an article *gives* it its value-in-exchange, yet it may be and often is true, in a certain sense, that the quantity of "labour" it contains is the *cause* of its having such and such a value in exchange.   But if ever we allow ourselves to use such language we must exercise ceaseless vigilance to prevent its misleading ourselves and others.

---

* Such psychological reactions as the desire to put one dish on the table in preference to another, simply because it is known to be more expensive, do not fall within the scope of this inquiry.

For what does it mean ?   The quantity-index and the curve
fix the value-in-exchange.   But the quantity-index may run
the whole gamut of the curve, and we have seen that what
determines the direction of its movement and the point at
which it rests is, in the case of freely producible articles,
precisely the quantity of "labour" contained in the article.
This quantity of "labour" contained, then, determines the
amount of the commodity produced, and this again determines the value-in-exchange.   In this sense the amount of
"labour" contained in an article is the cause of its exchange
value.   But this is only in the same sense in which the
approach of a storm may be called the cause of the storm-
signal rising.   The approach of the storm causes an intelligent
agent to pull a string, and the tension on the string causes
the signal to rise.   In this sense the storm is the cause of
the signal rising.   But it would be a woful mistake, which
might have disastrous consequences, to suppose that there is
any immediate causal nexus between the brewing of the
storm and the rising of the ball.   And if our mechanics
were based on the principle that a certain state of the atmos-
phere "gives an upward movement to a storm-signal," the
science would stand in urgent need of revision.   So in our
case : Relative ease of production makes intelligent agents
produce largely if they can ; increasing production results in
falling marginal utilities and exchange-values ; therefore, in a
certain sense, ease of production causes low marginal utilities
and exchange - values.   But there is no immediate causal
nexus between ease of production and low exchange-values.
Exchange values, high and low, are found in things which
cannot be produced at all ; and if (owing to monopolies,
artificial or natural) the intelligent agents who observe how
easily a thing is produced are not in a position to produce it
abundantly, or have reasons for not doing so, the ease of
production may coexist with a very high marginal utility,
and consequently with a very high exchange value.   In such
a case the amount of "labour" contained in the article will
be small out of all proportion to its exchange-value; and the
quantity produced may be regulated by natural causes that
have no connection with effort and sacrifice, or by the desire
on the part of a monopolist to secure the maximum gains.
Finally, there are certain phenomena, of not rare occur-

rence in the industrial world, which really seem at first sight to give countenance to the idea that the exchange-value of a commodity is determined, not by its marginal desiredness, but by the quantity of "labour" it contains. These phenomena are for the most part explained by the principle of "discounting," or treating as present, a state of things which is foreseen as certain to be realised in a near future. For instance, suppose a new application of science to industry, or the rise into favour of a new sport or game, suddenly creates a demand for special apparatus, and suppose one or two manufacturers are at once prepared to meet it. They may, and often do, take advantage of the urgency of the want of those who are keenest for the new apparatus, and sell it at its full initial exchange-value, only reducing their price as it becomes necessary to strike a lower level of desire, and thus travelling step by step all down the curve of quantity-and-value-in-exchange till the point of equilibrium is at last reached, and every one can buy the new apparatus who desires it as much as the "gold" that the same effort-and-sacrifice would produce. But it may also happen that the manufacturers who are already on the field foresee that others will very soon be ready to compete with them, and that it will require a comparatively small quantity of the new apparatus to bring it down to its point of equilibrium, inasmuch as it cannot, in the nature of the case, be very extensively used. They feel, therefore, that they have not much to gain by securing high prices for the first specimens, and on the other hand, if they "discount" or anticipate the fall to the point of equilibrium, and at once offer the apparatus on such terms as will secure all the orders, they will prevent its being worth while for any other manufacturers to enter upon the new industry, and will secure the whole of the permanent trade to themselves.

Any intermediate course between these two may likewise be adopted ; but the discounting or anticipation of the foreseen event only disguises and does not change the nature of the forces in action.

A more complicated case occurs when a man wants a single article made for his special use which will be useless to any one else. Let us say he wants a machine to do certain work and to fit into a certain place in his shop. The im-

portance to him of having such a machine is great enough
to make him willing to give £100 for it sooner than go
without it. But the "labour" (including the skill of the
designer) needed to produce it would, if applied to making
other machines, or generally to "gold-digging," only produce
an article of the exchange-value of £50. " In this case," it
will be said, " the marginal utility of the machine is measured
by £100, yet the manufacturer (if his skill is not a monopoly)
can only get £50 for making it, because it only contains
labour and other requisites to production represented by that
sum. Does not this show conclusively that it is the "labour"
contained in an article, not its final utility, which determines
its exchange-value ?" To judge of the validity of this objection, let us begin by asking exactly what our theory would
lead us to anticipate, and then let us compare it with the
alleged facts. We have seen that in equilibrium the marginal
utility of the unit of a commodity must occupy the same
place on the relative scales of all those who possess it ;
and further, that if ever that marginal utility should be
higher on A's relative scale than on B's, then (if B possesses
any of the commodity) the conditions for a mutually profitable exchange exist, though on what terms that exchange
will be made remains, as far as our investigations have taken
us, indeterminate, within certain assignable limits. Now if
we suppose the machine to be actually made we shall have
this situation : A, on whose relative scale the marginal
utility of the machine stands at £100 has not got it. B,
on whose relative scale it stands at zero, possesses it. The
conditions of a mutually advantageous exchange therefore
exist. But the terms on which that exchange will take place
are indeterminate between 0 and £100. When a single
exchange has been made, on whatever terms, then the
article will stand at zero on every relative scale except
that of its possessor, and no further exchange will be
made. If the machine exists, therefore, its exchange-value
will be indeterminate between zero and £100. Now if
we consistently carry out our system of graphic representation this position will be reproduced with faultless accuracy.
The curve of quantity-possessed-and-marginal usefulness with
reference to the community being drawn out, the vertical
intercept on the quantity-index indicates the exchange-value

of the commodity. Now in this instance the curve in question consists of the rectangle in Fig. 23 (*a*), where the unit on the axis of *y* is £100 per machine, and the unit on the axis of *x* is one machine. For the usefulness of the first machine to the community is at the rate of £100 per machine, and the usefulness of all other machines at the rate of 0 per machine. Therefore the curve falls abruptly from 1 to 0 *at* the value *x* = 1. But the quantity possessed by the community is one machine. Therefore the quantity index is at

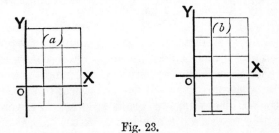

Fig. 23.

the distance unity from the origin, Fig. 23 (*b*). What is the length of the intercept? Obviously it is indeterminate between 0 and 1. This is exactly in accordance with the facts. Supposing the machine actually to exist, then, our theory vindicates itself entirely. But if the machine does not yet exist, what does our theory tell us of the prospect of its being made? We have seen that a thing will be made if there is a prospect of its exchange-value, when made, being at least as great as that of anything else that could be made by the same effort-and-sacrifice. Now the exchange-value is determined by the intercept on the quantity-index. Before the machine is made that intercept is 1 (= £100), but that does not concern the maker, for he wants to know what it *will be* when the machine is made, not what it is before. But it will be indeterminate, as we have seen, and therefore there is no security in making the machine. In order to get the machine made, therefore, the man who wants it must remove the indeterminateness of the problem by stipulating in advance that he will give not less than £50 for it. But what he is now doing is not getting the machine (which does not exist) in exchange for " gold." It is getting control or

direction of a given application of labour, etc. in exchange
for "gold," and this being so, it is not to be wondered at
that the price he pays for this "labour" should be propor-
tionate to the quantity of it he gets.

This is the general principle of "tenders" for specific
work.

We may appropriately close our study of exchange
value by a few reflections and applications suggested
by the ordinary expenditure of private income, and
especially shopping and housekeeping.

On p. 58 we considered what would be the most
sensible way of distributing labour amongst the various
occupations which might claim it on a desert island.
There labour was the purchasing power, and the question
was in what proportions it would be best to exchange it
for the various things it could secure. We were not
then able to extend the principle to the more familiar
case of money as a purchasing power, because we had
not investigated the phenomena of exchange value and
price. We may now return to the problem under this
aspect. The principle obviously remains the same.
Robinson Crusoe, when industrial equilibrium is established in his island, so distributes his labour that the
last hour's work devoted to each several task results in
an equivalent mass or body of satisfaction in every case.
If the last hour devoted to securing A produced less
satisfaction than the last hour devoted to securing B,
Robinson would reduce the former application of labour
till, his stock of A falling and its marginal usefulness
rising, the last hour devoted to securing it produced a
satisfaction as great as it could secure if applied otherwise. He would then keep his supply at this level, or
advance the supply of A and B together in such proportions as to maintain this relation. If he lets his stock
of A sink lower he incurs a privation which could be
removed at the expense of another privation not so
great; if he makes it greater he gets a smaller gratification at a cost which would have secured a greater

one if applied elsewhere. In equilibrium, then, the last
hour's work applied to each task produces an equal
gratification, removes an equal discomfort, or gratifies
an equal volume of desire ; which is to say, that Robinson's supply of all desired things is kept at such a
level that the unitary marginal utilities of them all
are directly proportional to the labour it takes to secure
them.

In like manner the householder or housewife must
aim at making the last penny (shilling, pound, or whatever, in the particular case, is the *minimum sensibile* *)
expended on every commodity produce the same gratification. If this result is not attained then the money
is not spent to the best advantage. But how is it to be
attained ? Obviously by so regulating the supplies of
the several commodities that the marginal utilities of a
pennyworth of each shall be equal. We take it that the
demand of the purchaser in question is so small a part
of the total demand for each commodity as not sensibly
to affect the position of its quantity-index on the national
register, and we therefore take the price of each commodity as being determined, independently of his
demand, on the principles already laid down. There is
enough lump sugar available of a given quality to supply
all people to whom it is worth 3d. a pound. Our housewife therefore gets lump sugar until the marginal utility
of one pound is reduced to the level represented by 3d.
Perhaps this point will be reached when she buys six
pounds a week. The difference between six pounds and
seven pounds a week is not worth threepence to her.
The difference between five pounds and six is. Sooner
than go without any loaf sugar at all she would perhaps
pay a shilling a week for one pound. That pound
secured, a second pound a week would be only worth,
say, eightpence. Possibly the whole six pounds may
represent a total utility that would be measured by

---

* *I.e.*, the smallest thing he can "feel." The importance of this
qualification will become apparent presently (see p. 129).

(12d. + 8d. + 5½d. + 4d. + 3½d. + 3d.) three shillings, or
an average of sixpence a pound, but the unitary marginal utility of a pound is represented by threepence.
Another housekeeper might be willing to give one and
sixpence a week for a pound of sugar sooner than go
without altogether, and to give a shilling a week for
a second pound, but her demand, though more keen, may
be also more limited than her neighbour's. She gets a
third pound a week, worth, say, sevenpence to her, and
a fourth worth threepence, and there she stops, because
a fifth pound would be worth less than threepence to
her, and there is only enough for those who think it
worth 3d. a pound or more. She has purchased for a
shilling sugar the total utility of which is represénted
by (18d. + 12d. + 7d. + 3d. =) 3s. 4d., but the unitary
marginal utility of a pound is 3d., as in the other case.

So with all other commodities. Each should be purchased in such quantities that the marginal utility of one
pennyworth of it exactly balances the marginal utility of
one pennyworth of any of the rest; the absolute marginal utility of the penny itself changing, of course, with
circumstances of income, family, and so forth, but the
relative utilities of pennyworths at the margin always
being kept equal to each other. The clever housekeeper
has a delicate sense for marginal utilities, and can
balance them with great nicety. She is always on the
alert and free from the slavery of tradition. She follows changes of condition closely and quickly, and keeps
her system of expenditure fluid, so to speak, always
ready to rise or fall in any one of the innumerable and ever
shifting, expanding and contracting channels through
which it is distributed, and so always keeping or
recovering the same level everywhere. She keeps her
marginal utilities balanced, and never spends a penny on
A when it would be more effective if spent on B; and
combines the maximum of comfort and economy with
the minimum of " pinching."

The clumsy housekeeper spends a great deal too much

on one commodity and a great deal too little on another.
She does not realise or follow the constant changes of
condition fast enough to overtake them, and buys
according to custom and tradition.   Her system of
expenditure is viscous, and cannot change its levels
so fast as the channels change their bore.   She can
never get her marginal utilities balanced, and therefore, though she drives as hard bargains as any one,
and always seems to "get her money's worth" in
the abstract, yet in comfort and pleasure she does
not make it go as far as her neighbour does, and
never has "a penny in her pocket to give to a boy,"* a
fact that she can never clearly understand because she
has not learned the meaning of the formula, "My coefficient of viscosity is abnormally high."

It is rather unfortunate for the advance of economic
science that the class of persons who study it do not as a rule
belong to the class in whose daily experience its elementary
principles receive the sharpest and most emphatic illustrations.   For example, few students of economics are obliged to
realise from day to day that a night's lodging, and a supper,
possess utilities that fluctuate with extraordinary rapidity ;
and the tramps who, towards nightfall, in the possession of
twopence each, make a rush on suppers, and sleep out, if the
thermometer is at 45°, and make a rush on the beds and go
supperless if it is at 30°, have paid little attention to the
economic theories which their experience illustrates.   As a
rule it seems easier to train the intellect than to cultivate the
imagination, and while it is incredibly difficult to make the
well-to-do householder realise that there are people to whom
the problem of the marginal utilities of a bed and a bowl of
stew is a reality, on the contrary, it is quite easy to demonstrate the general theory of value to any housekeeper who
has been accustomed to keep an eye on the crusts, even
though she may never have had any economic training.   For
the great practical difficulty in the way of gaining acceptance
for the true theory is the impression on the part of all but

---

* The absence of which was lamented by an old Yorkshire woman
as the greatest trial incident to poverty and dependence.

the very poor or the very careful that it is contradicted by experience. In truth our theory demands that no want should be completely satisfied as long as the commodity that satisfies it costs anything at all ; for in equilibrium the unitary marginal utilities are all to be proportional to the prices, and if any want is completely satisfied then the unitary marginal utility of the corresponding commodity must be zero, and this cannot be proportional to the price unless that is zero too. Again, since all the unitary marginal utilities are kept proportional to the prices, it follows that though none of them can *reach* zero while the corresponding commodity has any price, they must all *approach* zero together. Now all this, it is said, is contrary to experience. In the first place, we all of us have as much bread and meat and potatoes as we want, though they all cost something ; and in the next place, whereas the marginal utility of these things has actually reached zero, the marginal utility of pictures, horses, and turtle soup has not even approached it, for we should like much more than we get of them all.

We have only to run this objection down in order to see how completely our theory can justify itself ; but we must begin by reminding ourselves—first, that real commodities are not infinitely divisible, and that we are obliged to choose between buying a *definite quantity* more or no more at all ; and second, that our mental and bodily organs are only capable of discerning certain definite intervals. There may be two tones, not in absolute unison, which no human ear could distinguish ; two degrees of heat, not absolutely identical, which the most highly trained expert could not arrange in their order of intensity. With this proviso as to the *minimum venale** and the *minimum sensibile,* let us examine the supposed case in detail. A gentleman has as much bread but not as much turtle soup as he would like. This is bad husbandry, for he ought to stop short of the complete gratification of his desire for bread at the point represented by a usefulness of sixteen-pence a quartern (for we assume that he takes the best quality), and the surplus which he now wastefully expends on reducing

---

* The reply, "We don't make up ha'poths," which damps the purchasing ardour of the youth of Northern England, is constantly made by nature and by man to the economist who tries to apply the doctrine of continuity to the case of individuals.

that usefulness to absolute zero might have been spent on turtle soup. But let us see how this would work. We must not allow him to adopt the royal precept of eating cake when he has no bread, but must suppose him *bona fide* to save on his consumption of bread in order to increase his expenditure on turtle and on nothing else. Probably he already resembles Falstaff in incurring relatively small charges on account of bread—say his bill is 3d. a day. He has as much as he wants, and therefore the marginal utility is zero, but the curve descends rapidly, and if we reduce his allowance by one-sixth, and his toast at breakfast, his roll at dinner and lunch, and his thin bread-and-butter at tea, or with his whitebait, are all of them a little less than he wants, he will find that the marginal utility of bread has risen far above 1s. 4d. a quartern, and is more like a shilling an ounce. Taking the unit of x as 1 ounce, and the unit of y as 1d., it is a delicate operation to arrest the curve for some value between $x = 2\frac{1}{2}$, $y = 12$, and $x = 3$, $y = 0$. But let us suppose our householder equal to it. He finds that $x = 2\frac{3}{4}$ gives $y = 1$, and accordingly determines to dock himself of $\frac{1}{12}$ of his supply and save $\frac{1}{4}$d. a day on bread. But now arises another difficulty. He wants always to have his bread fresh, and the $\frac{1}{4}$d. worth he saves to-day is not suitable for his consumption to-morrow. The whole machinery of the baking trade and of his establishment is too rough to follow his nice discrimination. Its utmost delicacy cannot get beyond discerning between $2\frac{1}{2}$d. and 3d., and he finds that to be sure of not letting the marginal utility of bread down to zero he must generally keep it up immensely above 1d. per ounce. Suppose this difficulty also overcome. Then our economist saves $\frac{1}{4}$d. a day on bread or 6d. in twenty-four days. In one year and 139 days he has saved enough to get an extra pint of turtle soup, which (if it does not reduce its marginal utility below 10s. 6d.) fully compensates him for his loss of bread—but not for the mental wear and tear and the unpleasantness in the servants' hall which have accompanied his fine distribution of his means amongst the objects of his appetite. This is in fact only an elaboration of the principle laid down on p. 125.

As a rule, however, it is by no means true that we all have as much bread, meat, and potatoes as we want. Omitting all consideration of the great numbers who are habitually hungry, and confining our attention to the comfortable classes who always have enough to eat in a general way, we shall nevertheless find that the bread-bill is very carefully watched, and that a sensible fall in the price of bread would immediately cause a sensible increase in the amount taken. For instance, if bread were much cheaper, or if the house-keeping allowance were much raised, many a crust would be allowed to rest in peace which now reappears in the " resurrection pudding," familiar rather than dear to the schoolboy, who has given it its name ; but also known in villadom, where his sister uncomplainingly swallows it without vilifying it by theological epithets.

The assertion which for a moment seems to be true of bread, though it is not, is obviously false when made concerning milk, meat, potatoes, etc.   The people who have " as much as they want" of these things are few ; and if in most cases a more or less inflexible tradition in our expenditure prevents us from quite realising that we save out of potatoes to spend on literature or fashion, it is none the less true that we do so.   Indeed, there are probably many houses in which sixpence a week is consciously saved out of bread, milk, cheese, etc., for the daily paper during the session, when its marginal utility is relatively high, to be restored to material purposes when Parliament adjourns.

Before leaving the subject of domestic expenditure, I would again emphasise the important part which tradition and viscosity play in it.   This is so great that sometimes a loss of fortune, which makes it absolutely necessary to break up the established system and begin again with the results of past experience, but free from enslaving tradition, has been found to result in a positive increase of material comfort and enjoyment.

One of the benefits of accurate account-keeping consists in the help it is found to give in keeping the distribution of funds fluid, and preventing an undue sum being spent on any one thing without the administrator realising what he is doing.

A few miscellaneous notes may be added, in conclusion, on points for which no suitable place has been found in the course of our investigation, but which cannot be passed over altogether.

The reader may have observed a frequent oscillation between the conceptions of "so much a year, a month, a day, etc.," and "so much" absolutely. If a man has one watch, he will want a second watch less. But we cannot say that if he has one loaf of bread he will want a second loaf less. We can only say if he has one loaf of bread *a week* (or a day, or some other period) he will want a second less. Our curves then do not always mean the same thing. Generally the length on the abscissa indicates the breadth of a stream of supply which must be regarded as continuously flowing, for most of our wants are of such a nature as to destroy the things that supply them and to need a perpetual renewal of the stores provided to meet them. And in the same way the area of the curve of quantity-and-marginal-usefulness or the height of the curve of quantity-and-total-utility does not indicate an absolute sum of gratification or relief from pain, but a rate of enjoyment or relief per week, month, year, etc. Thus, strictly speaking, the value of y in one of our quantity-and-marginal-usefulness curves measures the rate at which increments in the *rate of supply* are increasing the *rate of enjoyment;* but we may, when there is no danger of misconception, cancel the two last "rates" against each other, and speak of the rate at which increments in the *supply* increase the *gratification;* for the gratification (area) and the supply (base), though rates absolutely, are not rates with reference to each other, but the ratio of the increase of the one to the increase of the other is a rate with reference to the quantities themselves.

We must remember, then, that, as a matter of fact, it is generally rates of supply and consumption, not absolute quantities possessed, of which we are speaking ; and especially when we are considering the conditions of the maintenance of equilibrium. It will repay us to look into this conception more closely than we have hitherto done ; and as the problem becomes extremely complex, unless we confine ourselves to the simplest cases, we will suppose only two persons, A and B, to constitute the community, and only two articles, V and W, to be made and exchanged by them, V being made

exclusively by A, and W exclusively by B. Let the curves on
Fig. 24 represent A's and B's curves of quantity-and-marginal-
utility of V and W; and let A consume V at the rate of q_{av} per
day (or month or other unit of time) and W at the rate of q_{aw},
while B consumes V at the rate of q_{bv}, and W at the rate of
q_{bw}. And let the position of the amount indices in the figure
represent a position of equilibrium. Let us first inquire how
many of the data in the figures are arbitrary, and then ask
what inferences we can draw as to the conditions for main-
taining equilibrium and the effects of failure to comply with
those conditions.

Since the quantities q_{av}, q_{aw}, etc. represent rates of consumption, it is evident that if equilibrium is to be preserved
the rate of production must exactly balance them. Now the
total rate of consumption, and therefore of production, of V
is $q_{av} + q_{bv}$, and that of W is $q_{aw} + q_{bw}$, calling these respectively q_v and q_w, we have

$$\text{(i)} \quad q_{av} + q_{bv} = q_v,$$
$$\text{(ii)} \quad q_{aw} + q_{bw} = q_w.$$

If we call the ratio of the marginal utility of w to that of
v on A's relative scale r, then we shall know, by the general
law, that in equilibrium the respective marginal utilities
must bear the same ratio on the relative scale of B; and if A's
curve of quantity-and-marginal-usefulness in V be $y = \phi_a (x)$,
and if $y = \psi_a(x)$, $y = \phi_b(x)$, $y = \psi_b(x)$ be the other three curves
then we shall have

$$\text{(iii) (iv)} \quad \frac{\psi_a(q_{aw})}{\phi_a(q_{av})} = \frac{\psi_b(q_{bw})}{\phi_b(q_{bv})} = r,$$

where $\phi_a(q_{av})$ etc. are the vertical intercepts on the figures,
and where each of the ratios indicated is the ratio of the
marginal utility of w to that of v on the relative scale. And,
finally, since B gets all his V by giving W in exchange for
it, getting r units v in exchange for one unit w, and since the
rate at which he gets it is, on the hypothesis of equilibrium,
the rate at which he consumes it (q_{bv}), and the rate at which
he gives W is the rate at which A consumes it (q_{aw}), we have

$$\text{(v)} \quad q_{bv} = rq_{aw},$$

and we suppose, throughout, that the consumption and pro-

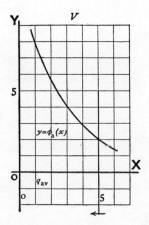
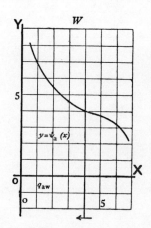
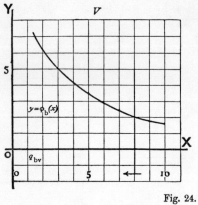
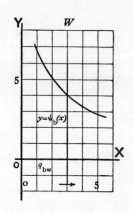

Fig. 24.

To face page 133.

duction go on continuously, that is to say, not by jerks, so that the conditions established are never disturbed.

Here, then, we have eleven quantities,

$$q_v, q_w, q_{av}, q_{aw}, q_{bv}, q_{bw}, \phi_a(q_{av}), \psi_a(q_{aw}), \phi_b(q_{bv}), \psi_b(q_{bw}), r,$$

and we have five relations between them. It follows that we may arbitrarily fix any six of the eleven quantities. Our five relations will then determine the other five.

Thus, if in the figures we assume that the four curves are known, that is equivalent to assuming that $\phi(q_{av})$, etc. are given in terms of q_{av}, etc., which reduces the number of our unknown quantities to seven, between which we have five relations. We may therefore arbitrarily fix two of them. Say $q_v = 13$, $q_w = 7$. We shall then have

$$\text{(i) } q_{av} + q_{bv} = 13,$$
$$\text{(ii) } q_{bw} + q_{aw} = 7,$$
$$\text{(iii) (iv) } \frac{\psi_a(q_{aw})}{\phi_a(q_{av})} = \frac{\psi_b(q_{bw})}{\phi_b(q_{bv})} = r,$$
$$\text{(v) } q_{bv} = r q_{aw},$$

which, if the meaning of $\phi_a(x)$ etc. be known, as we have supposed, gives us five equations by which to determine five unknown quantities. If $\phi_a(x)$ etc. were interpreted in accordance with the formulæ of the curves in the figure, these equations would yield the answers

$$q_{av} = 5,$$
$$q_{aw} = 4,$$
$$q_{bv} = 8,$$
$$q_{bw} = 3,$$
$$r = 2.$$

I do not give the formulæ, and work out the calculation, since such artificial precision tends to withdraw the attention from the real importance of the diagrammatic method, which consists in the light it throws on the nature of processes, not in any power it can have of theoretically anticipating concrete industrial phenomena.

Now suppose A ceases, for any reason, to produce at the rate of 13, and henceforth only produces at the rate of 10. The equilibrium will then be disturbed and must be re-established under the changed conditions. We shall have the same five equations from which to determine the distribution of V and W, and the equilibrium exchange value between them except that (i) will be replaced by

$$q_{av} + q_{bv} = 10.$$

If we wrote out $\phi_a(q_{av})$, etc., in terms of q_{av}, etc., according to the formulæ of the curves, we might obtain definite answers giving the values of q_{av}, etc., and r for equilibrium under the new conditions ; but without doing so we can determine by inspection the general character of the change which will take place.

If A continues, as before, to consume W at the rate of 4, giving V for it at the rate of 8, he will only be able to consume V at the rate of 2 himself, and the marginal utility of v will rise to more than half that of w.   He will therefore find that he is buying his last increments of W at too high a price, and will contract his expenditure on it, $i.e.$, the quantity index of q_{aw} will move in the direction indicated by the arrow-head.   But again, if A continues to consume V at the full present rate of 5, he will only be able to use it for purchasing W at the rate of (the remaining) 5, instead of 8 as now, and he will therefore get less than q_{aw}.   The marginal utility of w will therefore be more than twice that of v, and A will find that he is enjoying his last increments of V at too great a sacrifice of W.   He will therefore consume less V, and the quantity index will move in the direction indicated by the arrow-head, $i.e.$, A will consume less V and less W, and the unitary marginal values of both of them will rise.

But since we have seen that A gives less V to B (and receives less W from him), it follows that B, who cannot produce V himself, must consume it at a slower rate than before.   This is again indicated by the direction of the arrow-head on the quantity-index of q_{bv}.   Lastly, since A now receives less W than before there is more left for B, who now consumes it at an increased rate ; as is again indicated by the arrow-head of the quantity-index of q_{bw}.

Now since B's quantity-indexes are moving in opposite directions, and the one is registering a higher and the other a lower marginal usefulness, it follows that the new value of r will be lower than the old one. A's quantity-indexes, then, must move in such a way that the length intercepted on that of q_{av} shall increase more than the length intercepted on that of q_{aw}. Whether this will involve the former index actually moving farther than the latter depends on the character of the curves.

The net result is that though the rate of exchange has altered in favour of A, yet he loses part of his enjoyment of V and of W alike, while B loses some of his enjoyment of V, but is partly (not wholly) compensated by an increased enjoyment of W.

If we begin by representing the marginal usefulness of V and W as being not only relatively but absolutely equal for A and B, then the deterioration in A's position relatively to B's after the change will be indicated by the final usefulness of both articles coming to rest at a higher value for him than for B.

The only assumption made in the foregoing argument is that all the curves decline as they recede from the origin.

It should be noted—first, that we have investigated the conditions with which the new equilibrium must comply when reached, and the general character of the forces that will lead towards it, but not the precise quantitative relations of the actual steps by which it will be reached ; and second, that since the equations (iii) and (iv) involve quadratics (if not equations of yet higher order), it must be left undetermined in this treatise whether or not there can theoretically be two or more points of equilibrium.

The investigation of the same problem with any number of producers and articles is similar in character. But if we discuss the conditions and motives that determine the amounts of each commodity produced by A, B, etc. respectively, we shall be trespassing on the theory of production or "making."

Now, if we turn from the problem of rates of consumption and attempt to deal with *quantities possessed*, in the strict sense, without reference to the wearing down or renewal of the stocks, we shall find the problem takes the following form. Given A's stock of V, an imperishable article which both he and B desire ; given B's stock of W, a similar article ; and given A's and B's curves of quantity-and-marginal-desiredness for V and W alike ; on what principles and in what ratio will A and B exchange parts of their stocks ? The problem appears to be the same as before, but on closer inspection it is found that equation (v) does not hold ; for we cannot be sure that V and W will be exchanged at a uniform rate up to a certain point, and then not exchanged any more. Therefore we cannot say

$$q_{bv} = r q_{aw},$$

for in the case of *rates* of production, of exchange, and of consumption, every tentative step is reversible at the next moment. By the flow of the commodities the conditions assumed as data are being perpetually renewed ; and if either of the exchangers finds that he can do better than he has done as yet, he can try again with his next batch with exactly the same advantages as originally, since at every moment he starts fresh with his new product ; and if the stream of this new product flows into channels regulated in any other way than that demanded by the conditions of equilibrium we have investigated, then ever renewed forces will ceaselessly tend with unimpaired vigour to bring it into conformity with those conditions, so long as the curves and the quantities produced remain constant.   But when the stocks are absolute, and cannot be replaced, then every partial or tentative exchange *alters the conditions*, and is so far irreversible ; nor is there any recuperative principle at work to restore the former conditions.   The problem, therefore, is indeterminate, since we have not enough equations to find our unknown quantities by.   The limits within which it is indeterminate cannot be examined in an elementary treatise.   The student will find them discussed in F. Y. Edgeworth's *Mathematical Psychics* (London, 1881).

This problem of absolute quantities possessed is not only of much greater difficulty but also of much less importance than the problem of *rates* of consumption.   For when we are considering the economic aspect of such a manufacture as that of watches, for instance, though the wares are, relatively speaking, permanent, and we do not talk of the " rate of a man's consumption " of watches, as we do in the case of bread—or umbrellas,—yet the *manufacturer* has to consider the rate of consumption of watches per annum, etc., regarded as a stream, not the absolute demand for them considered as a volume.   Hence the cases are very few in which we have to deal with absolute quantities possessed, from the point of view of the community and of exchange values.   But this does not

absolve us from the necessity of investigating the problem
with reference to the individual, for he possesses some things
and consumes others, and has to make equations not only
between possession and possession, and again between consumption and consumption, but also between possession and
consumption.   That is to say, he must ask not only, " Do I
prefer to possess a book of Darwin's or a Waterbury watch?"
and, " Do I prefer having fish for dinner or having a cigar
with my coffee?" but he must also ask, " Do I prefer to
possess a valuable picture or to *consume* so much a year in
places at the opera ?" or, in earlier life, " Is it worth while
to give up *consuming* ices till I have saved enough to *possess*
a knife ?"   But these problems generally resolve themselves
into the others.   The picture is regarded as yielding a
revenue of enjoyment, so to speak, and so its possession
becomes a rate of consumption comparable with another rate
of consumption ; and the abstinence from ices is of definite
duration and the total enjoyment sacrificed is estimated and
balanced against the total enjoyment anticipated from the
possession of the knife.   If, however, the enjoyment of the
knife is regarded as a permanent revenue (subject to risks of
loss) it becomes difficult to analyse the process of balancing
which goes on in the boy's mind, for he seems to be comparing a *volume* of sacrifice and a *stream* of enjoyment, and
the stream is to flow for an indefinite period.   Mathemat-
ically the problem must be regarded as the summing of a
convergent series ; but if we are to keep within the
limits of an elementary treatise, we can only fall back
upon the fact that, however he arrives at it, the boy
" wants" the knife enough to make him incur the privations
of " saving up " for the necessary period.   He is balancing
" desires," and whether or not we can get behind them and
justify their volumes or weights it is clear that, as a matter
of fact, he can and does equate them.

This will serve as a wholesome reminder that we have
throughout been dealing with the balancing of *desires* of
equal weight or volume.   I have spoken indifferently of
" gratification," " relief," " enjoyment," " privation," and so
forth, but since it is only with the *estimated* volumes of all these
that we have to do the only things really compared are the
desires founded on those estimates.   And so too the " sense

of duty," "love," "integrity," and other spiritual motives all inspire desires which may be greater or less than others, but are certainly commensurate with them.   This thought, when pursued to its consequences, so far from degrading life, will help us to clear our minds of a great deal of cant, and to substitute true sentiment for empty sentimentality.   When inclined to say, " I have a great affection for him, and would do anything I could for him, but I cannot give money for I have not got it," we shall do well to translate the idea into the terms, " My marginal desire to help him is great, but relatively to my marginal desire for potatoes, hansom cabs, books, and everything on which I spend my money, it is not high enough to establish an ' effective ' demand for gratification."   It may be perfectly right that it should be so ; but then it is not because " affection cannot be estimated in potatoes ;" it is because the gratification of this particular affection, beyond the point to which it is now satisfied, is (perhaps rightly) esteemed by us as not worth the potatoes it would cost.   Rightly looked upon, this sense of the unity and continuity of life, by heightening our feelings of responsibility in dealing with material things, and showing that they are subjectively commensurable with immaterial things, will not lower our estimate of affection, but will increase our respect for potatoes and for the now no longer " dismal " science that teaches us to understand them in their social, and therefore human and spiritual, significance.

SUMMARY OF IMPORTANT DEFINITIONS
AND PROPOSITIONS CONTAINED
IN THIS BOOK.

I. One quantity is a function of another when any change in the latter produces a definite corresponding change in the former (pp. 1-6).

II. The total utility resulting from the consumption or possession of any commodity is a function of the quantity of the commodity consumed or possessed (pp. 6-8).

III. The connection between the quantity of any commodity possessed and the resulting total utility to the possessor is theoretically capable of being represented by a curve (pp. 8-15).

IV. Such a curve would, as a rule, attain a maximum height, after which it would decline ; and in any case it would *tend* to reach a maximum height (pp. 15-19).

V. If such a curve were drawn, it would be possible to derive from it a second curve, showing the connection between the quantity of the commodity already possessed and the rate at which further increments of it add to the total utility derived from its consumption or possession ; and the height of this derived curve at any point would be the differential coefficient of the height of the original curve at the same point (pp. 19-39).

VI. The differential coefficient of the total effect or value-in-use of a commodity is its marginal effectiveness or degree of final utility ; as a rule marginal effectiveness is at its maximum when total effect is zero, and marginal effectiveness is zero when total effect is at its maximum (pp. 39-41).

VII. For small increments of commodity marginal *effect* varies, in the limit, as marginal effectiveness (pp. 41-46).

VIII. In practical life we oftener consider marginal effects than total effects (pp. 46-48).

IX. In considering marginal effects we compare, and reduce to a common measure, heterogeneous desires and satisfactions (pp. 48-52).

X. A unit of utility, to which economic curves may be drawn, is conceivable (pp. 52-55).

XI. On such curves we might read the parity or disparity of worth of stated increments of different commodities, the proper distribution of labour between two or more objects, and all other phenomena depending on ratios of equivalence between different commodities (pp. 55-61).

XII. In practice the curves themselves will be in a constant state of change and flux, and these changes, together with the changes in the quantity of the respective commodities possessed, exhaust the possible causes of change in marginal effectiveness (pp. 61-67).

XIII. The absolute intensities of two desires existing in two different "subjects" cannot be compared with each other ; but the ratio of A's desire for u to A's desire for w may be compared with the ratio of B's desire for u or for v to B's desire for w (pp. 68-71).

XIV. Thus, though there can be no real subjective common measure between the desires of different subjects, yet we may have a conventional, objective, standard unit of desire by reference to which the desires of different subjects may be reduced to an objective common measure (pp. 73-77).

XV. In a catallactic community there cannot be equilibrium as long as any two individuals, A and B, possessing stocks of the same two commodities U and W respectively, desire or esteem u and w (at the margin) with unlike relative intensity (pp. 71-73).

XVI. The function of exchange is to bring about a state of equilibrium in which no such divergencies exist in the relative intensity with which diverse possessors of commodities severally desire or esteem (small) units of them at the margin (pp. 80-82).

XVII. The relative intensity of desire for a unit of any given commodity on the part of one who does *not* possess a stock of it, may fall indefinitely below that with which one or more of its possessors desire it at the margin without disturbing equilibrium (pp. 82-86).

XVIII. Hence in every catallactic community there is a general relative scale of marginal utilities on which all the commodities in the circle of exchange are registered ; and if any member of the community constructs for himself a relative scale of the marginal utilities, to him, of all the articles he possesses, this scale will (on the hypothesis of frictionless equilibrium) coincide absolutely, as far as it goes, with the corresponding selection of entries on the general scale ; whereas, if he inserts on his relative scale any article he does *not* possess, the entry will rank somewhere below (and may rank *anywhere* below) the position that would be assigned to it in conformity with the general scale.

And this general relative scale is a table of *exchange values.*

Thus the exchange value of a small unit of commodity is, in the limit, measured by the differential coefficient of the total utility, to any one member of the community, of the quantity of the commodity he possesses ; and this measure necessarily yields the same result whatever member of the community be selected (pp. 71-86).

XIX. As a rule exchange value is at its maximum when value-in-use is zero, and exchange value is zero when value-in-use is at its maximum (pp. 79, 80, 93-102).

XX. If we can indefinitely increase or decrease our supplies of two commodities, then we may indefinitely change the ratio between the marginal effects to us, of their respective units (pp. 108-124).

XXI. Labour, money, or other purchasing power, secures the maximum of satisfaction to the purchaser when so distributed that equal outlays secure equal satisfactions to whichever of the alternative margins they are applied (pp. 124-130).

INDEX OF ILLUSTRATIONS

THE END